ROBERTSON DAVIES

TWO PLAYS

Fortune, My Foe
&
Eros at Breakfast

Plays by Robertson Davies

Full length:

— *The King Who Could Not Dream*, written 1944, unproduced, unpublished.

— *King Phoenix*, written 1947, first production 1950. Toronto: New Press (in *Hunting Stuart and Other Plays*, edited by Brian Parker), 1972.

— *Benoni*, written 1945, produced by the Crest Theatre, Toronto, as *A Jig for the Gypsy*, 1954. Toronto: Clarke, Irwin, 1954.

— *Fortune, My Foe*, first production 1948. Toronto: Clarke, Irwin, 1949. New edition 1993.

— *At My Heart's Core*, first production for Peterborough's centenary 1950. Toronto: Clarke, Irwin, 1950; Toronto: Simon & Pierre, 1991.

— *Hunting Stuart*, first production 1955. Toronto: New Press (in *Hunting Stuart and Other Plays*, edited by Brian Parker), 1972.

— *General Confession*, never produced. Toronto: New Press (in *Hunting Stuart and Other Plays*, edited by Brian Parker), 1972.

— *Love and Libel*, adaptation of novel *Leaven of Malice*, Broadway production 1960. *Canadian Drama 7*, no. 2 (1981): 117-190, *Leaven of Malice: A Theatrical Extravaganza*.

— *Question Time*, first production at St. Lawrence Centre, Toronto, 1975. Toronto: Macmillan, 1975.

— *Pontiac and the Green Man*, performed at University of Toronto's sesquicentennial in 1975, unpublished.

One act:

— *Hope Deferred*, first produced 1948. Toronto: Clarke, Irwin (in *Eros at Breakfast and Other Plays*), 1949.

— *Overlaid*, first produced by the Ottawa Drama League 1947. Toronto: Samuel French, 1948; Toronto: Simon & Pierre, 1991.

— *Eros at Breakfast*, first production 1948. Toronto: Clarke, Irwin (*Eros at Breakfast and Other Plays*), 1949. New edition 1993.

— *The Voice of the People*, written 1949, Davies directed first production in 1950. Toronto: Clarke, Irwin (in *Eros at Breakfast and Other Plays*), 1949.

— *At the Gates of the Righteous*, first produced 1948. Toronto: Clarke, Irwin (in *Eros at Breakfast and Other Plays*), 1949.

Masques:

— *A Masque of Aesop*, performed 1952 at Upper Canada College. Toronto: Clarke, Irwin, 1952, 1955.

— *A Masque of Mr. Punch*, performed 1963 at Upper Canada College. Toronto: Oxford University Press, 1963.

Television Drama:

— *Brothers in the Black Art*, broadcast by CBC 1974. Vancouver: Alcuin Society, 1981.

ROBERTSON DAVIES

TWO PLAYS

Fortune, My Foe
&
Eros at Breakfast

 Simon & Pierre

We would like to express our gratitude to the Canada Council, the Ontario Arts Council, and the Ontario Publishing Centre for their support.

Kirk Howard, President; Marian M. Wilson, Publisher

1 2 3 4 5 · 5 4 3 2 1

Canadian Cataloguing in Publication Data

Davies, Robertson, 1913—
  Fortune, my foe ; & Eros at breakfast

ISBN 0-88924-241-0
  I. Title. II. Title: Eros at breakfast.

PS8507.A84F67 1992   C812'.54   C92-095703-X
PR9199.3.D3F67 1993

Cover Design: C.P. Wilson Graphic Communication
General Editor: Marian M. Wilson

Contents

Introduction
by Robertson Davies

When *Fortune, My Foe* was first produced by Arthur Sutherland's International Players in Kingston, Ontario, in August, 1948, there was little that might be called professional theatre in Canada. Since the latter days of the eighteenth century there had been touring theatre in the young colony, and companies, often of excellent quality, had visited Kingston from the United States and England, but the war of 1939-45 had put an end to that. Sutherland, who was an adventurous and charming man, thought that a professional company might survive in Kingston, and he called it International because it did indeed attract a good many visitors from the United States; they could come to Kingston from Watertown across the lake, have dinner at the Frontenac Hotel, in the ballroom of which the theatre was accommodated, see the play and be home by midnight. He gave them a diet of American and English comedies, as suitable summer fare, but he longed for something a little more daring—a Canadian play, in fact, at a time when Canadian plays were rarities—and he turned to me for one.

Arthur and I had been contemporaries and friends at Queen's University, in Kingston, and had often worked together in the students' Drama Guild. From his earliest days he was stage-struck. People often use that expression contemptuously, but I am not one of them; to yield to the beauty, the charm, the excitement and the profound psychological insight the theatre offers, is not to be a lightweight, an inconsiderable creature, but very possibly to be an artist, a creator, a person who enlarges and illuminates the lives of others. Even a simple run-of-the-mill comedy may offer charm and some excitement; beauty and psychology are less common, but that was what Arthur wanted. He knew it was risky, but he wanted a play about Canada.

It was risky because Canada has for a long time been thought a dull country, with dull people. But there was a time when Norway was thought dull, and Ireland was thought absurd, yet both of them brought forth plays which have been acclaimed as treasures by theatres around the world. I don't suppose for a moment that Arthur had any such ambition as that, but he thought Canada might have something to say, and he asked me for a play. I had written a few one-act plays, because those were what Canadian amateurs wanted, but something in three acts was a new venture for me.

What should it be about? When Arthur approached me I had already begun a play on the theme I have mentioned above—the supposed dullness of Canada and its poverty of artistic expression. We had poets, novelists, painters, and some of them were very good, but they seemed not to be accepted by Canadians as a whole in the way that other countries accept their artists. It was notorious that university teachers were poorly paid; perhaps it was thought that learning was its own reward. So there was my theme, and my hero was a young professor who loved his country and loved a girl, and received rather a frosty response from both of them. The character of the puppet-master, who brought the artistic feeling of the Old World to the New World, and met with indifference and sometimes incredulity, was everywhere to be observed in Canada at that time; the war had brought us many refugees, and we had not always understood what they could do or what they were that was important. The old professor, who had worn himself out in a university which he thought was beneath his deserts, and who projected his personal failure on the new country, was a familiar figure also, and not one to be wholly condemned, for Canada had not given him understanding. Oh, indeed, there was lots of material for a play; the problem was not to over-crowd the stage and load the play with that fatal thing, A Message.

Message was very much on the lips of Canadians like Philpott and Tapscott, the do-gooders who took up the puppet-show, without having any understanding of its special quality or its cultural background, but who were convinced that the task of art was to teach—to offer a Message, in fact, and to offer it in terms that the stupidest listener could understand. Canada was, and still is, full of such people. They think of art of all kinds as a sort of handmaid to education; it must have a Message and it must get it across.

The truth is that art does not teach; it makes you feel, and any teaching that may arise from the feeling is an extra, and must not be stressed too much. In the modern world, and in Canada as much as anywhere, we are obsessed with the notion that to *think* is the highest achievement of mankind, but we neglect the fact that thought untouched by feeling is thin, delusive, treacherous stuff.

A circumstance that lent distinction to Arthur's production was that the setting was from a handsome and imaginative design by Grant Macdonald. It is now in the Macdonald collection in the Agnes Etherington Art Gallery, at Queen's University in Kingston.

The play fulfilled Arthur's trust; it had an extended run, which was extraordinary, a theatrical wow, in Canadian theatre at that time. And it has been acted many times in Canada since, and I know that it has made a lot of people feel differently about Canada, because they have told me so. And that has been my reward, and a very welcome one.

The little play that appears also in this book, *Eros at Breakfast*, has an odd history. When I was a small boy in rural Canada, schools were expected to get up a concert at Christmas, and no concert was complete without a 'dialogue' or two. 'Dialogue' was the word used to describe a play suitable for children, always profoundly instructive, crammed with Message and just the sort of thing Philpott and Tapscott could understand and encourage. I was much impressed with one 'dialogue,' the scene of which was a human stomach. The Stomach was offered a variety of foods, and responded eagerly to Miss Piece-of-Cake (in those days the term had no ambiguous significance) and Mr. Slab-of-Pie, but these two characters proved false, and the Stomach suffered from their treachery. The Stomach found salvation with Mr. Apple and Miss Glass-of-Milk, highly virtuous characters, who brought peace, growth and improved intelligence with them to the owner of the Stomach.

Even as a child, I found this ghastly affair very funny (which was very wrong of me because dialogues were not meant to be funny in that way). And when I began to write plays, I thought that something that took place inside a human creature—in his solar plexus, for instance, where an astonishing complex of nerves at the base of the stomach does so much to influence our feelings and our minds—would be amusing. What would love do to the solar plexus of a young man newly in love? It would fill him with joy, and insane rapture, obviously. From there it was easy to conceive of the solar plexus as a government office, filled with civil servants who directed the affairs of the young man who incorporated it in his being— without really knowing that it existed.

This play also has had a wide acceptance, but it is a delusive little piece. It requires delicate comedy acting, and I have seen it done by actors who handled it too roughly. It is a fantasy, not something for Stunt Night at camp. I must add that I have also seen it performed in the spirit in which it is offered, and then it had its full effect, which is gently, and never unkindly, satiric.

Robertson Davies

Fortune, My Foe

Fortune, My Foe

Characters:
James Steele
Nicholas Hayward
Idris Rowlands
Edward Weir
Buckety Murphy
Franz Szabo
Vanessa Medway
Ursula Simonds
Mrs. E. C. Philpott
Orville Tapscott

Act One

(*The scene is James Steele's equivocal establishment near the city of Kingston, Ontario. It was built as the hangar for a small seaplane, and as it is early autumn the large doors at the back of the stage are open, and across the Cataraqui River the Kingston skyline may be seen in an autumn haze. Let no scene painter carelessly represent this by the usual huddle of flat roofs and false fronts which might serve as the skyline of most small Canadian cities: two cathedrals, a domed City Hall, the towers of limestone churches and a mass of river-shipping in the harbour make this one of the most picturesque prospects in Canada, and, in this light, one of the loveliest. It is late afternoon.*

The hangar has been floored, and is arranged as a simple cabaret; on the left the audience sees a counter which is almost a bar, but no bottles are visible, only soda water, pitchers of fruit juice, and a plate of oranges and lemons; behind this bar is a door to the proprietor's private quarters. On the right is a door from outside, from which two or three steps lead down into the room. Outside the big doors at the back a low, rough parapet marks the edge of the hangar floor, and the drop into the river. Three or four small tables, with chairs, are set about the room, and there are a couple of comfortable, but old-fashioned, deck chairs. The atmosphere of the place is clean and pleasant, but untidy.

The curtains part, slowly, upon a scene of impressive calm. At a table in the centre of the stage sits **Nicholas Hayward,** *reading a small, leather-bound book; he is of intellectual, but not owlish appearance, and is in his early thirties; he wears a tweed jacket and flannel trousers. Leaning upon the bar, in his shirtsleeves, watching* **Hayward** *with interest, is the proprietor of the place,* **James Steele,** *who is always called* **Chilly Jim;** *he is of middle age, muscular, keenly intelligent, and of strong individuality. In one of the chairs, asleep, is Professor* **Idris Rowlands;** *even when sleeping his appearance is noble, for he has the head of a sage or a poet. Outside the big doors at the back, brooding upon the distant prospect with his back to the audience, is* **Buckety Murphy,** *also called* **Bucket o' Slops;** *he is a bum, dissipated and frowsy; even on this warm day he wears a degraded overcoat and an unspeakable hat. When the audience has had a chance to drink in the peace and beauty of this scene, the actors may begin to speak.*

Nicholas *is the first to move; he makes a note on some paper which is on his table, takes a sip from the tall glass which is also there, and resumes his reading.*)

Chilly: Mr. Hayward, do you mind if I ask you a question?

Nicholas: Mm?

Chilly: What's that little book you've been reading all afternoon?

Nicholas: Joke book.

Chilly: Go on! Who ever saw a joke book bound in leather?

Nicholas: Why not?

Chilly: Because a book that's bound in leather is meant to last, and nobody wants a joke to last. I've sold joke books in my time, and they was always bound in paper.

Nicholas: This one was bound in paper when it was new, I suppose. When I bought it, it had no cover of any kind. I bought it when I was in England, during the war, and I paid sixpence for it. It is rubbish. And yet it is rare, too. Do you know, Chilly, that there isn't a library on this continent that has a copy of this book? I possess what may be the only copy between the North Pole and Cape Horn, and so I have had it handsomely bound, as you see, and I hope it may prove to be a treasure to me.

Chilly: Didn't you say it was rubbish?

Nicholas: Pitchblende is rubbish, but a precious substance may be refined from it, and I hope to get a fortune, or at least the foundation of a fortune, from this neglected book.

Chilly: You'll be luckier than a lot of others if you do. Professor Rowlands, there, told me once he'd written over a dozen books, and never made a cent out of any of 'em. He says the better a book is, the less money it will make.

Nicholas: Then I shall take care to write a very bad book. Anyway, the Professor doesn't like to think of someone succeeding where he has failed. It's human nature. Fail, and the world fails with you: succeed and you succeed alone.

Chilly: True enough. Take me, for example: by rights I should be a failure. I'm a self-educated philosopher and I'm a happy man. But you wouldn't believe the number of people that waste time worrying because I'm not in jail. Human nature's a caution. What's the name of your book?

Nicholas *(reading)*: "Nugae Venales, or a Complaisant Companion; Being New Jests, Domestic and Foreign, Bulls, Rhodomontadoes, Pleasant Novels, Lyes and Improbabilities collected by John Head: London 1686."

Chilly: Quite a name. The ones I used to sell were mostly "Captain Billy's Whizz-Bang" and that kind of thing. 1686—getting on for three hundred years ago. They must be old enough to be brand new by now.

Nicholas: No; that's exactly the point.

Rowlands *(waking)*: Have I been asleep long?

Chilly: Might be a couple of hours.

Rowlands: Hello, Nicholas. I didn't hear you come in.

Nicholas *(declaims)*:

>   Flow gently, Cataraqui
>   Among thy green braes;
>   Flow gently, I'll sing thee
>   A song in thy praise;
>   When Idris is asleep
>   By thy murmuring stream
>   We all go on tiptoe
>   To cherish his dream.

Rowlands: Very funny. What are you doing there? Is that the great work?

Nicholas: Yes, and coming along very nicely.

Chilly: What kind of jokes did they laugh at in 1686?

Nicholas: Well, here is one you may like. It is called "A Logical Quibble." Listen. "A merry fellow said he sung as well as most men in Europe, and thus he proved it: the most men in Europe do not sing well, therefore I sing as well as most men in Europe."

Rowlands: It seems to me I heard that on the radio last night.

Chilly: Any more as good as that in your book?

Nicholas: Oh, plenty. Listen to this one. "A gentleman that was baldheaded took great delight in hunting; one day he came hastily into the chamber of a friend who was seriously reading, and asked him if he would go hunt a hare. 'Pish,' said the other, 'let me alone; let them go and hunt hairs that have lost them.'"

Chilly: You know, Mr. Hayward, if you want my opinion, that's terrible.

Nicholas: Ah, but you are looking at it in the wrong way. People once laughed at these jokes, and we have no reason to suppose that people in 1686 were any sillier than people today. Indeed, I shall undertake to prove that at least two thirds of the jokes in this book, re-written and given a modern flavour, will make people laugh now. I shall do more: I shall find modern equivalents for these jokes, wherever possible, and print them with these seventeenth century originals. My edition of this old jest book will be a great new work on humour, and I shall write a preface—scholarly but not over the heads of ordinary men, and witty but not undignified—and my book will attract attention. I shall become known as a rising authority on humour. The *Reader's Digest* will ask me to run a monthly collection of old jokes, with explanations. I shall be a guest on the programs of famous radio funny men. And I shall get a great deal of money.

Rowlands: There's no money to be made by writing books. I know.

Nicholas: Not all of it will come from the book. That will merely be the cornerstone of my fortune. But I shall become known as a rising scholar in a little-explored field, and great American universities will fight for me.

Chilly: But you know, Mr. Hayward, I don't think it will work. You're a professor. People don't like funny professors. They don't trust them.

Rowlands: That's an old-fashioned point of view, Chilly. There was a time when a professor was a man who knew what ordinary people did not know, and they respected him for it. But your really up-to-date professor sticks his nose into the silliest manifestations of everyday life and tells the public that they are more important than they really are. In the States they have professors who specialize in the psychology of jazz, the social significance of the comic strips, or the effect of advertising on modern prose style. Nicholas, apparently, is going to join them. He means to become America's foremost academic buffoon.

Nicholas: There's no need for you to be so cutting about it. Don't you think that humour is worthy of serious study?

Rowlands: Yes, if the student is sincere. But you are only doing it to attract attention and get money. You can't use good means to reach a bad end.

Nicholas: Who said I was not sincere?

Rowlands: You said so yourself. You've got too much good stuff in you to waste it on nonsense and shoddy, catchpenny scholarship.

Nicholas: I think that you are the only man in the world I would allow to talk to me like that.

Rowlands: That is my Welsh gift. I should have been a preacher. I would have been a great preacher.

Nicholas: But you would not have been sincere.

Rowlands: Ah, but I would! If I could have caught and held the vision I had when I was twenty—Oh, hello, Ned.

(**Edward Weir** *has come in by the outside door; he is a newspaperman of pleasant appearance, somewhere between 35 and 45.*)

Weir: Hello, Idris. Hello, Chilly. You all look very domestic.

Chilly: What's the news?

Weir: If you want the news, you must see the evening edition of the Kingston *True Briton.* I don't know it. There is a widespread delusion that newspapermen always know the news. Now, I never know the news until I have read the evening paper. I spend my whole day digesting and writing comments upon yesterday's news, and I am always a day behind. And I'll tell you a secret: news bores me.

Rowlands: It bores me, too. The day's news so seldom touches upon anything really important.

Weir: News, as such, is a mass of unrelated accounts of violent and usually unpleasant occurrences. It is only interesting when a synthesis has been formed; that is my job. If any of you gentlemen feel inclined to write a letter to the editor of the *True Briton* saying how much you admire the editorials, I shall regard it as a personal favour.

Rowlands: I never read your damned editorials.

Weir: You would be a better man if you did. They would open up a wonderful new world to you.

Nicholas: What brings you here in the middle of the week, Ned?

Weir: One of the great problems of a Canadian bachelor is finding places where he can sit down and rest himself in peace. His boarding-house is intolerable, and in the homes of his friends he has to pay for his hospitality with a great deal of flattery and false gaiety. Chilly's place is the ideal bachelor's hang-out, as you very well know. It is never crowded, there are rarely any women, and the company, though mixed, is good.

Chilly: When I started this place, I said: "It's going to be a place where a man can be let alone. The world is full of fellows in search of surcease, and here's where they'll find it."

Nicholas: "In search of surcease." A fine phrase, Chilly. Sizzly, but fine.

Chilly: You know, Mr. Hayward, that language is my hobby.

Rowlands: In a teaching career which has extended over thirty-five years I have repeatedly advised students to read all the plays of Shakespeare in chronological order. Chilly is the only person that I know of who has taken that advice.

Weir: I'm definitely in search of surcease. I've had a bad day. What about it, Chilly?

Chilly: Orange or lemon?

Weir: Lemon.

(**Chilly** *quickly puts ice and sugar in a tall glass, and carefully adds a measure of lemon juice; he puts the glass on a tray with a small bottle of soda, and carries it to* **Weir**, *who is now sitting at* **Nicholas'** *table.*)

Chilly: Forty cents, please.

(**Weir** *pays him.* **Chilly** *then takes a boat hook from behind the bar, and goes through the doors at the back; he is seen to fish in the water with the hook.*)

Weir: This is the part I always like.

(**Chilly** *has fished up a dripping bucket, from which he takes a bottle of gin; he brings it to* **Weir**'*s table.*)

Chilly: Would you like me to *give* you some gin in that, Ned?

Weir: Why, thank you, Chilly; this is a delightful surprise.

Chilly *(pouring expertly)*: This is an absolutely legal and unbeatable system. I sell nice, fresh, healthy fruit drinks and if, when a friend comes in, I choose to give him something to put in his glass, who can complain about that? What's more, I never keep liquor on the premises. The river is Crown property— navigable water—any liquor found on it is probably Crown property, too. A beautiful, beautiful system.

Nicholas: But Chilly, if the police knew you gave everybody a drink that came here, I don't think you could explain it away.

Chilly: Yes, but I don't. Lots of people come in here, and all they get is a glass of lemonade. They never come back. It's my way of keeping the joint exclusive.

Rowlands: Some day the police will catch you, Chilly.

Chilly: Last time the police were here they dragged the river with grappling irons, and finally a fat sergeant dived in in his drawers. Didn't find a thing. Not a drop on the premises. They broke down a lot of hollyhocks looking around outside, and I sent them a bill, but they haven't paid me yet. You've got to have a very special mentality to be a cop. Not many flower-lovers among them.

Rowlands: While you have that bottle, you might as well give me another drink.

Chilly: Certainly, Idris. You see? Complete change of atmosphere. When you're lemonade customers it's Mr. This and Professor That. But when I am treating my friends an atmosphere of easy cordiality prevails. How about you, Nick?

Nicholas: Not now, thanks. Later, perhaps.

Rowlands: Nicholas must keep his faculties at their peak while he grapples with the humour of the seventeenth century.

Nicholas: Idris is angry with me because I am doing something that has never occurred to him. I am sorry to say that Idris can be very small about some things.

Weir: What's the trouble?

Nicholas: No trouble. I am writing a book, that's all. I am preparing an edition of this old jest book. (**Weir** *takes the book and looks at it.*) I hope to be able to prove that our sense of humour really changes very little. I shall make my book as amusing as possible, and I hope to sell quite a lot of copies.

Weir: And then what?

Nicholas: I discussed the matter with Dr. Caleb Peabody last spring at the annual meeting of the English Association. You know what that is, of course?

Weir: Vaguely.

Nicholas: It pretends to be a learned body, but it is really a great slave-market for scholars. The professors look us over and choose the ones they want for the year following. Peabody offered me a job for next year if—

Rowlands: If you wrote a book in the meantime. Scholars, like hens, must lay eggs at regular intervals if they expect anyone to keep them.

Nicholas: Vulgarly expressed, but substantially true. So I am writing a book to make a little reputation in hopes of getting a better job.

Rowlands: Damn these Americans, raiding our staffs. What did he offer you?

Nicholas: It would be rude to betray his confidence, Idris, but the figure was a flattering one. Hence the jest book.

Chilly: But the real trouble is that those jokes are no good.

Nicholas: Very few jokes are any good, but that does not hurt their popularity. Trace the variations of any sturdy joke: "Who was that lady I seen you with last night?" "That was no lady, that was my wife!" First variation: "Two musicians meet: 'Whose was that piccolo I seen you with last night?' 'That was no piccolo, that was my fife.'" Second variation: "An Eskimo woman came home to her igloo and found her husband frozen in a compromising posture with a beautiful stranger. Next morning at breakfast she asked him, 'Who was that lady I thawed you out with last night?'" You see? It is possible to go on and on, and the more luxuriantly the joke proliferates, the worse it grows. But it does grow, and that is my point. Very likely that joke goes back to the Middle Ages: "Says John-a-Nokes to John-a-Stile, 'Who was yon beauteous damsel I saw ye with yestere'en?' 'Nay, by St. Dunstan, 'twas no beauteous damsel, but mine own ill-favoured dame!'" A real joke is timeless and indestructible.

Weir: And not very funny.

Nicholas: You should know. Newspapers print jokes every day, and why?

Weir: To fill nasty little gaps at the bottoms of the columns.

Nicholas: Exactly. And yet there are scores of people who read every one.

Rowlands: Sometimes, by accident, I presume, and not by design, the same jokes appear two or three times in a single week.

Nicholas: And are read by the same people, with the same solemn expression, every time.

Weir: These aren't so bad, you know. Listen to this one: "A fellow walking in the dark held out both his arms to defend his face; coming against the door which stood out-right he ran his nose against the edge thereof; whereupon he cried out, 'Heyday, what a pox, my nose was short enough just now, and is it in so short a time grown longer than my arms?'"

Rowlands: That amuses you, does it?

Weir: Yes, and it would probably amuse you, too, if you weren't determined not to be amused.

Rowlands: This is not my laughing day. My prophetic mood is upon me.

Weir: Your prophetic mood always comes at the beginning of a new university year. Nothing brings out the Jeremiah in a professor like the thought of an entirely new group of virgin intellects bearing down upon him from the high schools of Canada. You are depressed by the idea of ravishing so much pretty innocence with your passionate scholarship.

Rowlands: Wrong; quite wrong. I am depressed by the fact that Nicholas means to use this book as the bait which will land him a job in the States.

Weir: I didn't know you hankered for an American job, Nicholas.

Nicholas: I don't particularly hanker for an American job, but I hanker for a little honour and a little money. These are things which Canada gives her scholars with the utmost reluctance, and usually when they are near unto death. In the States a scholar sometimes gets the sweets of life while he is still able to enjoy them.

Rowlands: Flesh-pots.

Nicholas: Who are you to talk about flesh-pots? You get the salary of a full professor, and I, after five years in the Army, get the salary of an instructor—the lowest form of academic life. Nine men stand between me and the modest competence which you enjoy, and every one of them must die, retire or get another job before I can hope for a salary on which I can travel, buy books, and live as a learned man should without looking at both sides of every nickel. You are one of them, and considering your character and habits, you are in splendid health. By strict actuarial reckoning, it will be twenty-two years and five months before I can hope for your job. By that time I shall be fifty-five, and my soul will be rust or gangrene.

Rowlands: Unless you are unusually lucky, your soul will be rust or gangrene at fifty-five, however much money you have.

Nicholas: You need an alkalizer, Idris. Chilly, give Idris two of those fizzy things in a glass. Now: how can I think of marriage on the money I'm getting? How—

(**Buckety** *has risen suddenly, and he comes into the room swiftly, with factitious enthusiasm, and hails the company.*)

Buckety: Gents, it's approaching! Did you hear them whistles? Five o'clock! Now, will some gent very kindly tell me exactly—exactly, mind you—when it is 5:02.

Weir: As a favour to you, Buckety. But the whistles must have been slow, for it's 5:01 now.

Buckety: Watch careful, Mr. Weir. Quiet, if you please, everybody. I'll explain everything in a minute. Just quiet, now.

(**Nicholas** *and* **Rowlands** *watch* **Buckety** *in amazement;* **Weir** *raises his hand;* **Buckety** *poises on tiptoe; there is a hush, and as* **Weir** *drops his hand,* **Buckety** *utters a strange, piercing, long-drawn cry.*)

Buckety: O-o-o-o-o-o-w-w-w-w-w!

Rowlands: Good God!

(*Only* **Chilly** *is unmoved; he watches with his arms folded upon the bar.*)

Buckety: That, gents, was my birth-cry. Forty-six years ago this instant I first saw the light of day. I have made it my custom, since reaching manhood, to celebrate the moment of my birth with a cry like that of a newborn child. Interesting, eh?

Weir: Astonishing.

Buckety: Make an unusual little piece for your newspaper, don't you think,

Mr. Weir.

Weir: Very unusual. Where do you think it ought to go? Social Notes?

Nicholas: Mr. Buckety Murphy, known to a large and choice circle as Bucket o' Slops, celebrated his sixty-ninth birthday yesterday by uttering a cry like a lake-steamer whistling for a pilot.

Buckety: Aw, now, not sixty-nine, Mr. Hayward. Call it the even sixty. And cause enough, I suppose, for a little celebration?

Rowlands: Can you give me one good reason, Buckety, why anyone should celebrate your birth? If you can I'll buy you a drink.

Chilly: No, he can't, and it's not his birthday anyhow. He's had a couple of birthdays already this year. There's moderation in everything.

Buckety: Well, not to put too fine a point on it, it may not be my strict birthday, but I'll tell you what it is. It's the anniversary of my wife's death, and unless I get a drink or two I won't be answerable. That's all. Not answerable.

Weir: Grief?

Buckety: Not really. Remorse, more like. She haunts me.

Nicholas: How?

Buckety: A misunderstanding, really, She had false teeth, y'see, upper and lower set, pure gold. Well, there was some kind of a misunderstanding at the time of the funeral, y'see, and I was out of my mind with grief, and the teeth disappeared. Now she must have got the idea that I hocked 'em, because every year, on this day, she comes and sort of gnashes at me, in my sleep. Only not really gnashing, see, because of no teeth; sort of an awful gumming. A terrible thing, gents; not a thing any man would wish an old soldier to go through, just for the price of a drink.

Weir: How many drinks do you suppose it will take to keep the gumming ghost at bay, Buckety?

Buckety: Oh, not more than one or two. Very little does the job for me.

Rowlands: Buckety has such an alcoholic fire banked down inside him that a couple of gins can stir it into a blaze. Give him one drink, Ned, and you'll have him roaring.

Buckety: Aw, Professor, that's a hard thing to say.

Rowlands: Go on, Buckety, your very sweat is 100 proof.

Buckety: Have your fun; I can take a joke. Ain't touched a drop today, and that's the God's truth.

Rowlands: Didn't I see you up an alley with a loaf of bread and a can of Sterno at two o'clock this morning?

Buckety: Just a loaf somebody give me. I et it before I went to bed.

Rowlands: He et it, he says! You heated the Sterno, poured it through the loaf to filter out the wax, and drank the goof. Don't think I don't know you, Buckety! You drink shoe polish, too, don't you?

Buckety: Not any longer, Professor. Makes your mouth dirty.

Rowlands: What about lilac hair tonic? Scents the breath very agreeably, I've heard.

Buckety: You're a great one for your joke, Professor. And now, please for sweet Jesus' sake, will you buy me a drink?

Rowlands: Give him one, Chilly. Make it a double.

Buckety: Ah Professor, you got a heart! You know better'n most I guess, how a man feels when he has to have a drink.

Weir: That's wiped your eye, I think, Idris.

Nicholas: A double gin is really cheap for the cruel fun you've had with old Bucket o' Slops, Idris. Did it make you feel good?

Rowlands: Look here, Nicholas, within the last few minutes you've suggested that my heart is gangrenous, you've told me that you are waiting for my job, and now you are finding fault because I offer Buckety a few pleasantries of the type which he best understands. Don't you think that your conversation is getting a little out of hand?

(Buckety has gone to the bar, where Chilly measures him out a double gin; offers lemon juice, which Buckety contemptuously rejects; Buckety seizes the glass, holds it aloft, and shouts.)

Buckety *(sings)***:**

> Now let us drink, a drink, a drink
> To Lydia Pink, a Pink, a Pink
> For she's a benefactress of the human race;
> For she invented
> A Vegetable Compound;
> And all the papers
> Publish her face.

(Very rapidly he pours a few drops into his palm, snuffs them up his nose, casts the remainder into his throat, gargles it noisily, swallows, shudders, and then suddenly appears to gain in candle-power and self-possession.)

Buckety: Thanks. I needed that.

Rowlands: Quite all right, Buckety. Many men feel the need of a restorative at this time of day.

Chilly: Now, Bucket o' Slops, you can stay here just long enough to get the smell of that off your breath, and then you get out. It's fellows like you that get philanthropists like me into trouble.

Buckety: Sure, sure, Chilly ol' man. Just whatever you say.

(He goes back to his lonely seat outside the doors, but this time he faces into the room.)

Nicholas: I'm sorry if I was nagging at you, Idris. I've been edgy for a day or two. Beginning of an academic year, I suppose.

Rowlands: No. You find fault with me because you are discontented with yourself. And you are discontented with yourself because of what you are doing there. You are not the man, Nicholas, to leave Canada for money.

Nicholas: Damn it all, why does everybody talk as though it were criminal for a scholar to want money? And what is sacred about the Canadian scale of payment for academic services? Is it disgraceful to want to make a name, to—to seek some recognition for whatever talents one many have?

Rowlands: Isn't it an odd thing to fight for a country, only to leave it for another?

Nicholas: I didn't fight for a country. Some men did, but I did not. I fought for an ideal, and that ideal is more honoured in the States than it is here.

Rowlands: The ideal of money, perhaps?

Nicholas: No, and you know that is not true. It is an ideal of civilization, an ideal in which a high standard of living means something more than merely a high standard of eating—

Rowlands: And you expect to find that in the States? The Americans are to the civilization of our day what the Romans were to the civilization of the ancient world: they are its middle-men, its popularizers, not its creators.

Nicholas: Yes, but behind all the commercialism and vulgarity there is a promise, and there is no promise here, as yet, for men like me. I am not patient! But I am not unreasonable! I can live on a promise, but in a country where the questions that I ask meet only with blank incomprehension, and the yearnings that I feel find no understanding, I know that I must go mad, or I must strangle my soul with my own hands, or I must get out and try my luck in a country which has some use for me!

Rowlands: You have a place here.

Nicholas: Despised because I do not teach anything useful. Despised because I want things from life which nobody else seems to miss. Despised because my abilities command so little money—

Rowlands: Money! Back to it again.

Nicholas: You speak of money with the easy disdain of a bachelor who has five thousand a year, and pickings.

Rowlands: If by "pickings" you mean fees for public speaking, summer school instruction, special lectures, and royalties for books, I consider the term tasteless and ill-chosen.

Weir *(rising)*: Good afternoon, Miss Medway.

(**Nicholas** *and* **Rowlands** *have been so absorbed in their wrangle that they have not noticed that for some time* **Vanessa Medway** *has been standing in the room, watching them with amusement; she entered by the door from outside. She is an attractive and beautifully dressed girl, but there is in her manner a mingling of hauteur, contempt, and consciousness of her own charm which makes many people dislike her.*)

Vanessa: You certainly do raise your voice when you're angry, Nicholas—especially when you're angry with Canada. Hello, Professor Rowlands. Hello, Ned. Hello, Chilly. Sorry to intrude, when I know you don't like women here, but I had to see Nicholas. Nicky, darling, I want you to take me to the dance at the Yacht Club tonight. I've decided I want to go, and all the men who can dance have girls already. You don't mind, do you?

Nicholas: No; no, of course I'll take you. What about tickets and all that?

Vanessa: I've got them. I thought I'd pick you up so that you could get dressed.

Rowlands: If I may ask, Miss Medway, what made you think of looking for him here?

Vanessa: The logical place; it's where all men come to get away from women.

Rowlands: Now that you're here, will you have a drink?

Vanessa: I don't drink, thanks.

Weir: Cigarette?

Vanessa: You know I don't smoke, Ned.

Rowlands: Chilly has some delicious fruit juice.

Vanessa: No, Chilly doesn't like women here. He thinks they give the place a bad name. As soon as Nicholas is ready, I'll go.

(She expects **Chilly** *to say something of a gallant nature, but he continues to look at her with stony disapproval.)*

Nicholas: I can go anytime, I suppose.

Vanessa: No, don't let me tear you away from a fascinating argument. What was he shouting about so loudly, Professor?

Rowlands: Nicholas has been bitten by the emigration bug. He thinks his future lies in the U.S.A.

Vanessa: Oh, the book? I expect it will sell by the millions. There are a lot of awfully rude jokes in it—the very frank kind with dirty words in them, and lots of them about privies. Have you ever noticed how people who can't bear jokes about sex love jokes about privies?

Nicholas: Wouldn't it be a good idea to have a sandwich or something here before we go? Then we won't have to fuss about dinner.

Vanessa: I'll wait if you want to eat something. I'm not hungry.

Chilly: She doesn't drink; she doesn't smoke; she doesn't eat. What do you do, lady?

Vanessa: Well, Chilly, I used to attend the university. Now I just hang about waiting for some man to come along and marry me. Sometimes I think I'll get a job. Men like girls with jobs; it seems to give them a sense of security. What are you going to eat, Nicholas?

Chilly: I can give you ham or beef sandwiches, lettuce, radish, and a banana and some coffee. How's that?

Vanessa: That'll be splendid. Give him beef sandwiches, and I'll change my mind and have coffee, too. Oh, and another banana, if you have it.

Weir: You are one of the few people I know, Vanessa, who could eat a banana with elegance.

Vanessa: I believe there is a way of doing it so that you never touch the flesh; it's a method of wrapping the skin, but I don't know it. I just gobble.

(**Buckety** *makes another one of his quick sallies into the room.*)

Buckety: Would anybody like company while they eat? Lady, I've got something very interesting I could show you.

Vanessa: No thank you.

Nicholas: Run away, Buckety.

Buckety: Honest lady, I haven't had anything but the suckings of a hollow tooth since yesterday. For a sandwich I'd do you a real favour.

Nicholas: Get along, Buckety.

Buckety: It's photographs. Wouldn't sell 'em for a million, but I'll give 'em to you for a sandwich, because you got a lucky face.

Nicholas: Go on! Get out!

Vanessa: Nicky, don't drive him away. Nobody ever tried to sell me dirty photographs before.

Buckety *(indignant)*: They ain't dirty; they're artistic!

Weir: That's what they all say, Buckety.

Rowlands: You have an unfortunate presence, Buckety; it does not inspire confidence. I think it's that hat. Or possibly you have a disagreeable breath. The art of salesmanship depends upon such details.

(**Chilly** *has brought in the food, which he places on the table for* **Nicholas** *and* **Vanessa***; he jerks his head at* **Buckety***.*)

Chilly: There's some stuff in the kitchen for you, Buckety. Eat it up and get out.

Buckety: Aw, Chilly, you're white. I always say it. Whitest fellow in this damn, lousy town. And a prince! A white prince!

A Voice: Good Afternoon. Good afternoon ladies and gentlemen!

(**Buckety** *has been making his way toward the kitchen, talking over his shoulder; he has arrived at the bar as the Voice speaks, and he turns to find an odd little man sitting on the bar, almost under his nose. It is* **Mr. Punch**, *as he appears in the Punch and Judy shows. His appearance startles all the company.*)

Buckety: Holy God!

Punch: I'm happy to see you all looking so well. Aren't you glad to see me? Oh, deary, deary, deary, deary, what a pretty young lady! Won't you give me a kiss, my dear? Your young man won't mind. All the girls love me because I'm so handsome!

(**Punch** *shakes his head hysterically, and laughs; then a hand reaches up from behind the bar and hits him over the head with a stick; he disappears with a shriek. Then* **Franz Szabo** *stands up behind the bar; he is a European of middle age, somewhat shy, and when he speaks his address is in sharp contrast to the forward manners of Mr. Punch.*)

Szabo: Hello. I hope I am not making a nuisance with my little joke?

Rowlands: I haven't seen Punch since I was a boy. Are you going to give a show?

Szabo: Oh no, I don't think.

Chilly: Listen, Franz, I didn't tell you to start a floor-show. Go on back and wash some dishes.

Szabo: I have done all that.

Chilly: Well, polish some glasses. Don't come scaring everybody with that animal.

Szabo: Is not an animal. Is very famous Mr. Punch. But I do what you say right away. Sorry to have intruded, really I am.

Vanessa: No, don't go away. Let me see Punch. Isn't he a darling? What a wonderful face!

Szabo: He is very old. About a hundred years, I think it. Very old English figure. He has been my companion for many, many years, and now he comes to Canada with me. Eh, Mr. Punch?

Punch *(waving arms, and singing)*: Oh Canada, my home and native land—

Vanessa: Oh, he's sweet!

(**Buckety** *has gone unobtrusively into the kitchen.*)

Punch: No, I am not sweet. I am a very bitter and melancholy fellow! Oho! Oho! Pop goes the weasel!

Vanessa: Oh, do let me have him! Let me see if I can make him work!

Szabo: Oh, no, dear young lady, I cannot let you do that!

Vanessa: Why not?

Szabo: I cannot explain, really. But I cannot. He would not like it. Nobody ever makes him live but me, you see? Yes?

Vanessa: No, I don't see, really, I won't hurt him. Are you afraid I will do something stupid?

Szabo: No, no, no; I do not want to be rude; really I don't. But if he were a violin, now, or a cello, you would understand.

Vanessa: Don't you think there is a difference? A doll is not a violin, is it, and you are not quite a violinist, are you?

Szabo: Oh, now I have hurt your feelings.

Vanessa: No, you haven't hurt my feelings at all. But I think you are being rather pretentious. You will be telling me next that you are an artist.

Szabo: But I am—or rather, I was. I know I must seem very foolish. People have been so good as to call me an artist—foolish, perhaps. Franz Szabo is my name. In Prague I was quite well known.

Weir: I saw some puppets in Prague ten or twelve years ago.

Szabo: Really? There are many puppet shows there.

Weir: I've never forgotten them. I never thought that anything could be so enchanting. Would you have been in Prague at that time?

Szabo: Oh yes; my family and their puppets have been in Prague for three hundred years. When Shakespeare was writing plays in England, Szabo's Bohemian Puppets were well known.

Weir: I think that must have been the outfit I saw. In a tiny little theatre near the Ring?

Szabo: Yes, that was the one.

Weir: I'll never forget it. Somehow it seized on my imagination as very few things in life ever do. Say, you're a great man! Will you have a drink?

Szabo: Oh, I don't think—perhaps not—I am working for our good friend you see.

Nicholas: Are you going to show your puppets in Canada?

Szabo: Yes, I hope—after a time, when I can get together a troupe.

Weir: Oh, isn't your company with you?

Chilly: He's on his uppers. I gave him a job washing dishes.

Szabo: I hope you will not say anything. It would not be good if anyone kn
where I am.

Chilly: He's in a jam. Got to lie low for a while.

Weir: What's the trouble? Maybe I could help?

Szabo: Oh, is a very complicated matter. I am a Displaced Person, you see. There came a chance to come to Canada and I took it, and for a while I was in bush work north of Montreal. Then I become ill, you see, and it is pneumonia, and they send me to hospital in Montreal, and the doctors see that I am older than I said. Then I get a lot of papers from Ottawa, and they say I must be re-considered, you see, and maybe I have to go back. So when I get out of hospital I disappear.

Chilly: Friend of mine had him tucked away last time I went there for supplies.

Szabo: It is a terrible thing to lie to a government. They do not want old people here; of course I understand about that. But I do not want to go back. And I do not feel so very old.

Rowlands: That is the tragedy of age; no one ever really feels old.

Szabo: So I am hiding, you see, and I hope that maybe they will forget about me.

Weir: If you hope to give shows in public, how can you expect to remain hidden?

Szabo: Oh, a new name; I dye my hair.

Weir: Dangerous. Have you got those papers with you? The ones that came when you were in the hospital?

Szabo: Yes, I did not like to throw them away.

Weir: Let me see them

Szabo: Yes, of course.

Vanessa: Have you any more dolls with you?

Szabo: Dolls? The puppets, you mean? No, I have only Mr. Punch.

Nicholas: Do you expect to give Punch and Judy shows here?

Szabo: No, no; the Punch and Judy are hand-puppets; I never use them except for amusement for myself. I work with true marionettes—the figures with strings—very carefully made. They are truly—expressive; they become alive. For the real marionette master, you see, the figure must become an extension of himself; while he works, it must be more real than himself. That requires a fine figure. Mr. Punch is a very dear friend, but he is not a marionette.

Punch: No, no; Mr. Punch is a devil. Ha ha ha ha!

Szabo: I have a few pictures of my marionettes which I lost in Europe, if you would like to see them, dear young lady.

Vanessa: Yes, I'd like to see them very much.

Weir: I'd like to see those papers now, if I may.

Szabo: Yes.

Vanessa: We'll go with you, and Ned can look at the papers while you show me the pictures.

Nicholas: Yes, I'd like to see them too.

Vanessa: No, you stay here, Nicky, and eat your sandwiches. You can see the pictures some other time. We've got to get away soon. You have to dress, and then I must dress, and that will take a long time. So eat up like a good boy while I look at pictures.

Nicholas: Vanessa, I wish you wouldn't treat me as if I were five years old.

Vanessa: I know. It's horrid of me, isn't it? I only do it to be tiresome.

(**Vanessa, Weir** *and* **Szabo** *go out through the door behind the bar;* **Buckety** *returns from the kitchen, replete, and goes to his old place on the parapet by the water;* **Chilly** *removes the banana skin which* **Vanessa** *has left, and pours himself a cup of coffee at the bar.)*

Rowlands: Chilly, may I have a cup of your excellent coffee?

Chilly: Right away. Like anything to eat, Professor?

Rowlands: Not unless you are making something for yourself.

Chilly: No. I did a lot of cooking this morning, and I got full up with the smell of it.

Nicholas: Chilly lives on the smell of his own cooking, as Jehovah was supposed to exist on the smell of burnt offerings.

(**Chilly** *has brought* **Rowlands** *his cup of coffee, and he now takes the pot out into his kitchen, leaving* **Nicholas** *and* **Rowlands** *there alone.*)

Rowlands: Vanessa is a charming girl, isn't she?

Nicholas: Yes.

Rowlands: When she was at the university she attended a number of my courses. An interesting mind. Remarkably detached. I sometimes wondered that science did not appeal to her more than the arts.

Nicholas: Really?

Rowlands: Have you known her long?

Nicholas: For some time.

Rowlands: You mustn't be annoyed by the way she bosses you around, you know. She does that hoping that you will show temper.

Nicholas: I think I know her well enough to look out for myself.

Rowlands: Ah, really? Well, do you think you know her well enough to change the course of your life for her? You want to marry her, don't you?

Nicholas: What business is that of yours?

Rowlands: Everything that concerns humanity about which I can possibly get first-hand information is my business. Don't be stupid. I shall find out some way or other, and it might as well be directly from you.

Nicholas: What do you care about it?

Rowlands: I delight in such things. I want to know as much as possible about the affairs of as many people as possible. I see you violently wrenching your life out of one course in order to set it on another for a girl. What would you think of me if I were not curious about it? Would you think I was a gentleman, too well-bred to be inquisitive? No, you would think that I was an egotistical fool, too concerned with the impression he gave to the world to take any interest in the world itself. When a man loses his curiosity he has lost the thing which binds him to humanity. I wonder how much you know about Vanessa Medway?

Nicholas: I don't want to discuss her with you.

Rowlands: The more fool you, because I might be able to tell you a few things you don't know. She charms you, I suppose, by her cool and assured air? By the impression she gives that everything in life amuses her—slightly? That is very engaging in so young a woman, isn't it? But you think that it is superficial, and that Vanessa can be transformed into a very different woman, and that you are the man to do it. You think that she will always be aloof and amused toward the world, but that toward you she will be the fulfilment of your heart's desire. Ice to the world and fire to you?

Nicholas: Shut up, Idris. You're going too far.

Rowlands: Don't talk like an officer in some imaginary nineteenth century mess, Nicholas. I know Vanessa, and I know her father, too. She is something more than a match for you, my boy.

Nicholas: Idris, are you presuming to advise me from your own experience? Upon what you have learned from the genteel, decayed vestals who provide companionship for a man like you in a university town? I have heard you, in your cups, compare your development as a poet with that of Shelley: am I now to be shown some fascinating parallel between you and Byron? Which of us knows better what my needs are? What courses I must follow? What inexplicable jumps I must make from what you can understand to what you can't?

Rowlands: I understand better than you think.

Nicholas: You flatter yourself.

Rowlands: No; you undervalue me.

Nicholas: That has been your complaint about the whole world.

Rowlands: And a just complaint. My real gift is for something which this age, and particularly this country, undervalues.

Nicholas: Interesting. What is it?

Rowlands: Talk. You smile. Everyone smiles when they do not laugh outright. But it is true. I have failed as a writer, but as a talker I am an artist. Canadians do not understand or like good talk. They call me a windbag. It is as though a jury of Ontario housewives condemned Helen of Troy because she was not their equal in bottling pickles.

Nicholas: You dignify your Welsh gift of the gab with the name of art, do you?

Rowlands: Yes, and to get back to where this began, listen to me: because my finest flights of poetry are verbal and extempore, and not committed to paper, you deny me the name of poet. But I am a poet, Nicholas, and I have a poet's insight, compared with which the probings of the psychoanalyst are clumsy and futile.

Nicholas: Very well; to calm you I grant you a poet's insight. But I do not grant you the right to poke your nose into my affairs.

Rowlands: Fool! What is poetry but poking a nose into every man's affairs? I am not yet an old man, but I have seen enough of the world—seen it with deep understanding—to know that men like you have a predisposition to fall in love with women like Vanessa Medway—women who attract love only that they may reject it, and whose greatest pleasure is to wipe their feet on what better women would give their hearts for!

Nicholas: Oh, come, Idris; I was angry with you, but now I see that you are merely ridiculous. What a melodramatic description of an extremely charming, rather inexperienced girl.

Rowlands: Don't mistake sophisticated inexperience for innocence. Medusa was inexperienced, I suppose, before she turned her first man to stone; but the power and the urge were in her.

Nicholas: Rubbish!

Rowlands: You are too vain of your individuality, Nicholas. You think that nothing can happen to you as it has happened to other men.

Nicholas: I think that other men have won happiness through love and bold action, and if moving a few hundred miles into another country can be called bold action, I mean to take it.

Rowlands: To get money. Isn't it? She won't have you unless you have money?

Nicholas: Let's change the subject.

Rowlands: Then I am right? It is money she wants?

Nicholas: I admit nothing. But ask yourself, Idris, how a man and his wife would live on what I get.

Rowlands: Others do it.

Nicholas: More fools they.

(Chilly *returns, big with news.)*

Chilly: You should see the pictures Franz has of his theatre! All kinds of plays, real scenery, wonderful clothes, and the dolls—he can make them do anything! He has some pictures from a magazine, that show the whole place as it was before the war, and the dolls acting "Don Coyote." Looks wonderful! And in one of the pictures Franz is standing with a doll about two feet high, and you can see how he works it: strings—about twenty strings—and he says you have to touch them just as lightly as you'd touch the strings of a harp when you make it whisper. I wouldn't have believed it! Of course, I've never seen anything like that, and I don't suppose many people have on this side of the water. I'm going to help him get a theatre like that going here.

Rowlands: I don't think I've ever seen you so enthusiastic about anything before, Chilly.

Chilly: I can be enthusiastic when I see a good reason for it. And I'm a great man for novelty. Sometimes it seems to me that I've seen just about everything there is to see: murder, for instance—I've seen three murders done. But I've never seen anything that appealed to me like this!

(Enter **Weir** *and* **Vanessa,** *with* **Szabo** *following, from behind the bar.)*

Weir: You fellows ought to have a look at Szabo's pictures. He's the right man; I mean the man whose puppets I saw in Prague.

Rowlands: Yes, Chilly has just been rhapsodizing about them.

Vanessa: It's the most perfect thing you ever saw. A miniature theatre, tiny people—a whole world of make-believe.

Weir: No, I wouldn't call it that. When you see it in action the effect is one of intensified reality, rather than of make-believe. You know when you look at people through the wrong end of binoculars how clear and fresh and marvellously detailed everything seems to be? It's like that.

Rowlands: Chilly is about to astonish us with a new aspect of his genius. He says he is going to help our friend here to start a puppet theatre in Canada.

Chilly: That's right. Just as soon as it's safe for him to show his face. Or maybe on the quiet. I have a natural affinity for working on the Q.T. A little theatre here, now, would draw quite a crowd, and nobody need ever know who pulls the strings.

Weir: No, it will be best to get everything straight at Ottawa before doing anything. I've looked at Szabo's papers, and I know a man in the Department of Immigration who might be able to do something for us.

Szabo: You are all most kind. It is very good of you to be interested so much in my marionettes.

Chilly: Well, what are we waiting for? How long would it take to get ready for a show, Franz?

Szabo: Working hard, and with good luck, I think perhaps two years.

Chilly: Two years! That's quite a while.

Szabo: There is very much to do.

Vanessa: We'll help you, of course. I want to be one of the people who works the puppets. But I don't know that I can wait for two years; I might have changed my plans by then. Couldn't I begin now?

Szabo: If you begin tonight, and work every day for two years, perhaps—I say perhaps—you will be able to work a puppet well enough to put him on the stage after two years.

Vanessa: To work it as well as you, yes. But to work it well enough for an audience that doesn't know much about puppets; that shouldn't take more than a month or so.

Szabo: I began when I was eight years old, but my father would not let me put a puppet on the stage until I was sixteen. And I was not a master until I was twenty-four. So you see it took me sixteen years to become a master. You could not make your arms strong enough in less than six months. To hold a marionette very delicately, and to make tiny movements with him—that takes an arm like a—what do you say?—the man who makes iron things—a blacksmith! Feel my arm.

Vanessa: I think you'll find that things move a little faster in this country.

Szabo: I know. This is the Atomic Age! And this America! That is why I say two years to make a puppeteer.

Rowlands: Where do you expect to find a group of people to work that long just to make dolls dance?

Weir: Oh, now Idris, that's not quite fair; this is something more than dancing dolls.

Rowlands: To most people, I think, it will appear as dancing dolls.

Szabo: I do not know where they will come from. But they will come.

Vanessa: You are very sure.

Szabo: There were marionettes in Egypt long ago; there were marionettes in

Rome. There have been marionettes ever since. There must have been people
to make them act. Why should I think that there are no such people in Canada?

Rowlands: We have the talkies in Canada. Have you heard of them?

Szabo: Oh, yes. But somebody discovered Coca Cola, and there is still a place
for good wine, is there not? You do not understand the psychology of the
immigrant, I think, Professor Rowlands. This is my country now—if Mr. Weir
can help me to stay here. I *must* be hopeful. I *must* believe in it, for there is
nowhere else for me to go.

Rowlands: I was an immigrant myself, once.

Szabo: From England, I think? And a professor? That is different. No; I cannot
judge Canada, and examine all her faults. For me there is only hope—or
despair. I must hope.

Weir: That's the way to talk.

Szabo: And hope will do great things.

Chilly: You're right. Here's a man with faith. Not booster's faith, or
blabbermouth faith, but real faith. Now what are we going to do for him?

Weir: Well, I'll begin by seeing what I can do to make it possible for him to
stay in Canada. Meanwhile, Szabo, you'd better stay here and keep out of sight
or the R.C.M.P. may pick you up.

Chilly: I'll look after him. But couldn't you get to work on a show? Make a
few puppets or something like that while you're waiting?

Szabo: Oh yes. Though I must make puppets for a play. They are not like real
actors who can appear in a dozen plays.

Nicholas: Would you like me to write you a play?

Szabo: It is most kind of you to offer. I think I would like a new play very
much. Something that marionettes could do.

Nicholas: I'll think about it and talk to you tomorrow.

Vanessa: Aren't you being rash, Nicky? You've never written a play, and you have your book to finish.

Nicholas: I can manage it easily. I want to help.

Vanessa: I want to help, too, but Mr. Szabo is rather hard to help. He won't even let me hold Mr. Punch.

Szabo: But you see—

Nicholas: Oh, don't make a mountain of a molehill, Vanessa.

Vanessa: I don't mean to. But the book means a great deal to you, and it might mean quite a lot to me. I don't think you should do anything foolish.

Rowlands: I don't quite see how I can help. But I might suggest a play to you, Nicholas. What about a dramatization of "The Golden Asse," by Apuleius?

Nicholas: That's a brilliant idea! I'll look at it tonight.

Vanessa: I don't think I know it. What is it about?

Rowlands: It is about a man who is turned into a jackass by a woman who does not understand the nature of her own enchantments. Then he does a lot of foolish things before he comes to himself.

(Both **Nicholas** *and* **Vanessa** *try to think of some suitable comment on this remark, but there is none; after the slightest awkward pause, they decide to behave as though it had no significance.)*

Vanessa: We ought to be going, Nicky.

Nicholas: I suppose so. I'll think about the play, Szabo. Good luck in the meanwhile.

Szabo: Thank you.

Chilly: We ought to have a drink to Franz and his puppets.

Vanessa: No thank you; we really haven't time.

(At the word "drink," as by magic, **Buckety** *joins the group.)*

Punch: I have time! I have time! O Canada! Oh hurrah! Here's to me! Here's to the famous Mr. Punch! Here's to all the woodenheads! Ha ha ha ha ha!

(He has seized a tumbler from the bar, and lifts it repeatedly to his mouth. **Chilly, Rowlands, Buckety** *and* **Weir** *lift coffee cups, glasses, or whatever they may have in his direction. As the curtain falls,* **Mr. Punch** *throws his glass triumphantly on the floor.)*

(Curtain)

Act Two

(A week has passed. Through the large doors of **Chilly**'s *converted hangar an autumn sunset fills the room with warm light. As the Act progresses the electrician may amuse himself by changing this to dusk, and then to a fine autumn night.*

> *The room is much as it was before, though the producer may wish to alter the positions of the tables and chairs in order to make new groupings possible.* **Franz Szabo** *is sitting in a chair, shaping the limb of a new puppet; he wears a carpenter's apron, in which he catches the shavings, and he works, slowly, minutely, and with deep concentration. He is not so preoccupied, however, that he cannot talk to* **Buckety**, *who sits near him, and who addresses him with the patronage of a native toward a foreigner.)*

Buckety: Y'know, Franz, I been watching you. You're a good worker. You're slow, but you don't make any mistakes. With luck, you ought to go a long way.

Szabo: Thank you.

Buckety: Yeah, with luck, and some good advice. Maybe you need a manager.

Szabo: Perhaps.

Buckety: This side isn't like the Old Country, y'know. Got to keep your eyes wide open.

Szabo: Aha?

Buckety: Competition's deadly.

Szabo: So?

Buckety: It's our economic system. Capitalism.

Szabo: Ah, yes?

Buckety: Severe, mind you. Weeds out the unfit. You either go up or down. Root hog or die.

Szabo: Really?

Buckety: The pace is killing. But the rewards are great.

Szabo: Yes?

Buckety: Fortunes made in a day. Lost overnight. Millions changing hands all the time.

Szabo: Extremely interesting.

Buckety: Look at me, for instance. You'd never believe the money that's been through these hands. Mind you, I'm not complaining. I'm pretty well retired now.

Szabo: So I understand.

Buckety: But in my palmy days—! Now listen, Franz, I like you.

Szabo: You are very good to say so.

Buckety: I've always been a quick judge of character, and I like you. But you've got one bad fault. You won't mind me telling you what it is?

Szabo: Which of my bad faults do you mean?

Buckety: You're a dreamer, that's it. This isn't a country for dreamers.

Szabo: No country ever is.

Buckety: I was a dreamer too, once. You mightn't think it, but it's true. When I was a young fellow I had a wonderful physique. I used to pose for photographs, in a leopard skin, or sometimes stark naked, kind of sideways. I was superb. I don't mind saying it because it's the truth: I was lovely.

Szabo: Astonishing!

Buckety: Lemme show you. I got a set of pictures I posed for at the height of my career. *(He fishes an envelope of cards from the folds of his garments.)* See here: this series was called "The Toilet of Hercules"— Hercules was a strong Greek, y'know. These were made for a stereopticon; they're not very common now; that's why there's two pictures on each card. Lookit; here I am, y'see, with a lion skin on, and my club and holding a fake bear on my back. Then here I am, y'see, holding the club so as to show muscles. And here's Hercules with his lion skin half off drinking from a stream; that's to show leg and back muscle. Then here's Hercules taking off the skin and combing his hair; I had a wealth of hair and moustache, as you can see. Then here's Hercules, bare as a bird, with his back to the camera, waving goodnight to the stars; sort of Greek saying his prayers, y'see? Then here's Hercules asleep, dreaming of the chase, with every muscle tense and showing just about everything, y'see. That was my apex, so to speak.

Szabo: This is quite remarkable. And who bought the pictures?

Buckety: Oh, everybody. Artists, for the body. And women for the artistic content. And boys who wanted to build themselves up to be like me, y'see. Biggest sale was to women.

Szabo: And what happened?

Buckety: Oh, I made a lot of money, and I decided to go into business for myself. Wanted to expand the appeal of the photographs, so I began to reac out toward women. That was a mistake.

Szabo: Yes, so often it is.

Buckety: Got some girls to pose; "The Toilet of Venus" as a kinc opposite number to my Hercules, y'see, and then "Venus and Mars." was the finish. Distributed them very carefully, of course, through pri agents, and only to trusted persons. But somehow the cops got holɗ set, and that was the end of a high class artistic venture. And all be< I was a dreamer, and wanted to give the public what was too good But I want you to profit by my mistakes, Franz, because I haven'i mean or jealous bone in my body.

Szabo: I am sure of it.

Buckety: The money I've handled in my time! Thousands and thousands! Might as well call it millions. All gone, now. All gone because I was too much the artist. But the experience remains. And experience is just like money in the bank. Now, do you know what you need?

Szabo: A man of experience to help me?

Buckety: Right! I didn't expect you to say that. But since you realize it, that makes everything easier. You need a manager. Now, do you know what's wrong with this puppet scheme of yours?

Szabo: What is wrong with it?

Buckety: It's got to be streamlined. It's old stuff; horse and buggy stuff. That's one thing. And the second is this: you're in the wrong place. Canada's no country for show business. There's just one place for you, and that's Hollywood!

Szabo: Oh no!

Buckety: Now listen, Franz: I take you to Disney, see, and I say, "Walt, I want you to see what Franz can do." Then you show him your stuff. Then I say, "Walt, you and I know that this is a gold-mine; how are we going to bring this up to date? Franz just wants to be told." Then we work it all out, and you're in. But it would take handling. You couldn't tackle it yourself.

Szabo: But Buckety, even if I wanted to do that, I could not. I cannot go to United States. I am not a Canadian. I am not even an Austrian any more. I was born a Bohemian, but that is all gone. I am nothing. I am lucky to be here, and here is where I shall stay.

Buckety: That end of it'll take working out. I'll have to get in touch with Ottawa about that. Leave it to me.

Szabo: You are very kind, but please don't bother.

Buckety: Say, Franz, I'm a bit short at the moment. You couldn't lend me a couple of hundred, could you?

Szabo: Not a couple of dollars.

Buckety: I'd let you have my note of hand, of course.

Szabo: Not a cent.

Buckety: Oh well.

(He seems to collapse sadly inside his clothes. **Idris Rowlands** *enters by the outside door; he has been walking and he carries a rough walking stick and wears a crushed hat of vaguely sporting character.)*

Rowlands: Hello there. Has old Bucket o' Slops been trying to borrow money?

Szabo: How did you know?

Rowlands: Where two are gathered together, and one of them is Buckety— I know the signs.

(Buckety *slinks away to the back, where he sits and surveys the sunset. After a time he goes to sleep.)*

Szabo: Poor fellow. He wants to be my manager. I who have nothing.

Rowlands: I sometimes wonder why Chilly lets him hang around.

Szabo: Chilly is a very good man, in some ways. Did you ever visit any of the monasteries in Europe? They always had one or two sad people about them. Cripples, or half-wits or fellows like poor Buckety. I think it was to remind the brothers that life could be cruel, and that some misfortune might bring them to a similar condition. Do you think Chilly lets Buckety stay here to show his other customers what drink can do if it becomes the master of a man?

Rowlands: I never thought of that. Yes. I've seen those chaps hanging about monasteries but I never thought of them as living sermons. It seems to me that evil grows and proliferates like cancer, without any strict or discernible justice, striking blindly. Smug people say that character is destiny; they might say with equal sense that destiny is character. I knew Europe well, before the war. Went there every summer.

Szabo: You knew Prague, I expect?

Rowlands: Very well. Or perhaps I shouldn't say very well, since I never heard of your famous theatre.

Szabo: Oh, that is nothing.

Rowlands: On the contrary. You seem to have filled Edward Weir with a holy fire. Setting you up in Canada is all he thinks about now. During the last week there have been two editorials in the *True Briton* about the poverty of our country's artistic life; some day he won't be able to hold in any longer, and will burst into an impassioned demand for puppets. What his publisher will think I don't know.

Szabo: You joke.

Rowlands: As for Nicholas Hayward, all he thinks about is writing plays for you. He has no less than four themes, I understand, and can't make a choice among them.

Szabo: I know. Just as a precaution I am working on my old favourite, Don Quichotte. This is one of his arms.

Rowlands: The enthusiasm of youth! Sometimes it makes me sigh; sometimes it makes me spew. They think it can do anything.

Szabo: Perhaps that is good.

Rowlands: We need not deceive ourselves, you and I. We are of the same generation. Don't think I despise your puppets. I can see that they give the whole delight and mystery of the theatre in miniature, and that like so many things which we enjoy in miniature they have a special, piercing sweetness. But do you think that they can appeal to the Canadian blockheads?

Szabo: Not all blockheads, surely?

Rowlands: I have taught in a Canadian university for twenty-five years. How many generations is that? How many students? I don't know. I have faithfully unlocked the treasures of a great literature for them all, and in all those years, and among those students, do you know how many I found who had wit enough to know what wealth I offered? Three, Szabo, three! And they are all three in the States, now. Do you wonder that I do not want Hayward to go? God, how I tried to love this country! How I tried to forget the paradise of Wales, and the quick wits of Oxford! I have given all I have to Canada—my love, then my hate, and now my bitter indifference. This raw, frost-bitten country has worn me out, and its raw, frost-bitten people have numbed my heart.

Szabo: A numb heart would not feel so much because a young man of talent was going to leave his native land. If you were truly indifferent to Canada, you would not care how its brilliance bled away.

Rowlands: I see that you are a very reasonable man, Szabo. Well, I am not reasonable. Because I am a professor silly people suppose that my line is thinking. It isn't; it's feeling.

Szabo: You are an artist, then.

Rowlands: I might have been an artist. But I played safe and became a teacher. That's fatal. Contact with the young and their perpetual curiosity soon kills the spark in a man. Teaching means forever going back to the beginning again. An artist must press on. Hayward might do fine things.

Szabo: He has been most kind to me. Mr. Weir has been very good, too, and he loves the theatre, but Mr. Hayward has given me great encouragement. He has great sympathy about the marionettes. It is not just imagination, you know, that they do not like to be handled by anyone but the master. He can understand that. Miss Medway does not understand. She is helping me too, but she does not understand. Mr. Hayward encourages me to think that in time I shall make a place for my puppets in Canada. He says so.

Rowlands: That's too bad of him.

Szabo: Why?

Rowlands: Because it isn't true. We don't have to pretend to each other, Szabo; we are of the same generation. You'll never be able to do anything with your puppets here.

Szabo: You do not think so?

Rowlands: I'm sorry, but I know so. Your little people are for an audience wiser and less frost-pinched than any you will find here. Don't break your heart, man.

(**Nicholas Hayward** *comes in by the outside door.*)

Nicholas: Good evening, Idris. Hello Franz, what are you making there?

Szabo: A part of Don Quichotte.

Nicholas: I wish I could make up my mind about your play. I'll do you a version of "Don Quixote" if you like, but I'd rather tackle something less hackneyed.

Rowlands: I've just been talking to Szabo about his chances here, Nicholas. I think it's cruel of you and Weir to lead him on. You know as well as I do what chance he'll have in this country. If he had a sophisticated entertainment which he could do in night-clubs he might get a little work here, but all he has is an old world puppet show, and he'll never persuade the new world to like it.

Nicholas: I think he will. He's going to do things like "Don Quixote" and "Dr. Faustus." They'll go very well, I think.

Rowlands: Where?

Nicholas: We haven't gone into that very thoroughly yet. After all, the idea is only a week old.

Rowlands: You do not intend to go across Canada as advance agent, I suppose? No, of course not. You and Weir are filling Szabo full of enthusiasm for a project which appeals to you. You are urging him to give Canada something which you think Canada needs. But when it comes to the real work, the heartbreak, the poor audiences and the failure, neither of you will be there.

Nicholas: You're obsessed by the idea of failure, Idris.

Rowlands: Aha! And are you setting up as an optimist? You're getting out of Canada as soon as you can, I observe.

Nicholas: Are we going to quarrel about that again?

Rowlands: Why not? Canada is good enough for Szabo, and you foresee a comfortable future for him with his box of dolls. But you can see no future here for yourself. Szabo isn't a fool. Don't you suppose he wonders why you fill him up with stories about the opportunities of a country when you mean to turn traitor to it yourself?

Nicholas: Traitor! It's impossible to talk to you! Since when has a man been a traitor because he looked for what he wanted outside his homeland! There is more than one loyalty, as you should know. If loyalty to an ideal of civilization takes me away from Canada, what about it?

Rowlands: How fortunate that this admirable loyalty takes you in the direction of big money.

Nicholas: To the States, you mean? I would be far happier if it were taking me to England.

Rowlands *(ironically)*: Oh, indeed?

Nicholas: Yes. You know my feeling for England. Nothing would make me happier than to live there.

Rowlands: I know your feeling for England. It is a sentimental attachment, on a high literary level, for a country which has never existed anywhere but in the minds of romantic young men from the dominions.

Nicholas: Don't forget that I've lived in England.

Rowlands: Yes, as an undergraduate and as a soldier. But that is a very different thing from being born there and having to make your way there. Your childhood was spent in Canada, and your notion of England is still that of a child in love with romantic reading. Your England is all lions rampant, stagecoaches, Ann Hathaway's cottage, Kenilworth Castle, and Christmas cards by Raphael Tuck.

(Szabo, *embarrassed, slips away unnoticed into the kitchen.*)

Nicholas: From one student of English literature to another, that is rather a remarkable accusation.

Rowlands: Oh no. You have read so much English literature that you expect every farm hand in England to talk like a character in Hardy, and every English soldier to have the patriotism of Shakespeare at his brassiest. Your ideal of civilization! It's a sentimental schoolboy's longing for a land which never existed, and never will exist!

Nicholas: Thank you for this frank appraisal of my intelligence.

Rowlands: Oh, I know you educated Canadians! I know your hunger for a land better than your own! And I know how green it makes the dales of England seem! And it's the same with the States; when you want money you can always find a reason for going there—a fancy reason, that's to say.

Nicholas: You are convinced that nothing but money could lure me to the States.

Rowlands: And am I not right?

Nicholas: You think that I would give up my British heritage, and my allegiance to a monarchy which I honour in my mind and love in my heart, for money and nothing else?

Rowlands: Aha, has the moment come now when you are going to tell me, with a pretty blush, that you are going to do it for love?

Nicholas: And is that a bad reason?

Rowlands: Yes. No girl who really loved you would insist on so much sacrifice to prove it. But Vanessa Medway likes to find out how much men will sacrifice for her; it enables her to compute her own value.

Nicholas: Listen, Idris; if you weren't too old and too flabby I'd give you the sock on the jaw you've been asking for ever since I came in. But you pay attention to what I say: I want you to keep out of my affairs from now on, and I don't want to hear you mention Vanessa's name.

Rowlands: Perhaps I have been a little bitter. But I only wanted to give you some advice.

Nicholas: To hell with your advice! Oh, you can talk wisely enough, when you choose, but every word you say is tainted by everything you are. Do you think I don't know what's behind your scorn for England and the States? You never were asked to go to the one, or to return to the other. You're a sour, frustrated old man, jealous of any success that comes to others. You whine about your failure as a teacher in Canada, and hint that Canadian stupidity caused it. No, no, Idris; lay not that flattering unction to your soul; your failure came from within. And like every pulpy old mess who has botched his life, you are full of bitter wisdom which you are only too eager to offer to the young. I don't want any of it. In men like you the heart withers many decades before the faculties decay, and the process feels like the coming of wisdom. But real wisdom is sound and ripe, and yours is neither, for wholesome fruit doesn't grow on a cankered tree.

(**Rowlands** *looks at him and* **Nicholas** *returns his gaze without relenting; deeply humiliated,* **Rowlands** *rises, takes his hat and stick, and goes to the door. As he is leaving,* **Vanessa** *comes in with her friend* **Ursula Simonds**, *a woman some years older than she, and marked by that curious aloofness which distinguishes the zealot.* **Rowlands** *does not return their greetings, nor does he appear to notice them.*)

Vanessa: Good evening, Professor Rowlands. How odd! Nicky, didn't you think that he was looking rather strange? I always thought he liked me. Has anything happened?

Nicholas: Oh, he's all right. Thinking of something else and didn't notice you, I suppose.

Vanessa: I don't think it's very nice of you to suggest that people can overlook me so easily. You know Ursula, don't you?

Nicholas: We've met. How do you do?

Vanessa: Ursula is terribly interested in our little puppet man. She wants to see what he can do.

Nicholas: Oh? I shouldn't have thought that puppets were much in your line, Miss Simonds.

Ursula: Everything is in my line, one way or another. He's a Czech, isn't he?

Nicholas: Or an Austrian, or a Bohemian. Like a lot of people he doesn't know quite what he is, any longer.

Ursula: Quite. He should present a very interesting problem.

Nicholas: Oh, I wouldn't call him a problem. That's the one thing he is determined not to be.

Ursula: You know what I mean: new horizons open before him; he must adjust himself; his re-orientation creates a problem. What will Canada do to him?

Nicholas: What will he do to Canada?

Ursula: Exactly! In every immigrant there is hope. Some of them bring nothing but the rags and tatters of the old world. But others bring the shining promise of the world that is to be.

Nicholas: I see.

Vanessa: Ursula is terribly serious. Do you wish I took more interest in politics, Nicky?

Ursula: Vanessa thinks that politics is just a hobby. But she has a very open mind.

Vanessa: Where's Franz?

Nicholas: He was here five minutes ago. I suppose he slipped away into the kitchen.

Vanessa *(at the kitchen door)*: Franz! Come here, will you? A friend of mine wants to meet you.

Ursula: I have never been here before. It's a sort of informal club, isn't it?

Nicholas: No. Open to the public, more or less.

(**Szabo** *enters, still carrying his work.*)

Szabo: Good evening. How nice to see you.

Vanessa: Ursula, this is Franz Szabo. Franz, this is Miss Ursula Simonds. She wanted to meet you. I've told her about your puppets, and what you are going to do here, and everything, and she's terribly interested.

Szabo: Oh? You are interested in puppets?

Ursula: Very much. You keep up with all the latest developments, of course.

Szabo: Puppets have not really changed for hundreds of years. The puppet master develops, but the puppets are the same.

Ursula: That's what I mean. But the old toy can be put to new uses.

Szabo *(gently)*: If you call a marionette a toy, perhaps you call a violin a box.

Ursula: I didn't mean to insult you. But you know that they think of marionettes as toys.

Szabo: Do they? Who are they?

Ursula: Most people. Call it the middle class, or whatever you like. The uninstructed majority. They never look below the surface. Whatever your marionettes say to them, they accept goodnaturedly. But what the puppet says, sticks in the mind, and particularly in the child mind. Do you follow me?

Szabo: No.

Ursula: Well, to take an example at random, marionettes have been very widely used in the U.S.S.R. to make Soviet ideas clear to children and simple people who would not understand a lecture or a book. I was reading a very interesting article about that just the other day.

Szabo: So?

Ursula: Some of the plays are very funny. But the lesson is always plain. What plays are you going to do with your puppets?

Szabo: Oh, some of the old ones: "Don Quichote," and "Dr. Faust," I suppose. And I hope for some new ones, perhaps about Canada. And I always like to have a little revue in my repertoire, with songs, and clowns, and funny animals, and such, you know.

Ursula: Excellent. Perhaps I could help you with some songs and a play or two.

Szabo: Oh, you write plays?

Ursula: I'd like to try.

Szabo: Even a play for puppets is not easy.

Ursula: But the principal thing is to have something to say, don't you agree? Your message is what makes your play. Get your message first, then clothe it in some little fable—the simpler the better—and there is your play.

Szabo: Aha, and you have a message?

Vanessa: Oh, Ursula has a lot that she wants to say. That's why she wanted to get in touch with you.

Ursula: Yes; when Vanessa mentioned you I saw that this was a splendid opportunity to do some work for the enlightenment of the Canadian people. This is a politically backward country, you know. I am sure that in Europe you were acquainted with causes, perhaps even active in them, which were in advance of the general run of political thinking here. Now you people from Europe have a great opportunity to bring enlightenment to your new land. You, in particular, have a means of helping to bring Canadians up to date in their political thinking.

Szabo: So?

Ursula: And I'm sure you see what a good joke it would be to bring a new message under the disguise of something as old and apparently childlike as a puppet show.

Szabo: I am sorry. I do not like that kind of joke. And, I thank you very much, I do not want to join the communist movement here. I would be no use to it,

I assure you, Madame.

Ursula: Communist? I said nothing about communism.

Szabo: No, but—

Ursula: Whenever any kind of political advance is mentioned, there are people who shout about communism. But I am not a communist.

Szabo: Then I am very sorry. I have seen a great deal of communism in Europe, and perhaps I am foolish about it. I have been approached by communists before in this country, and they talked very much like you.

Nicholas: A surprising number of people think that you are a communist, Miss Simonds. It is strange how such impressions gain ground.

Ursula: I make no secret of my beliefs. They are advanced—too advanced for many ill-informed people. But I am most certainly not a Party member.

Szabo: In any case, I can be of no help to you. I know nothing about politics. And I would not be happy teaching politics with my puppets.

Ursula: Do you not recognize a purpose in life which is higher than being happy?

Szabo: No. I am sure that is very old-fashioned, but it is true.

(**Chilly** *has come in, and during the last two or three speeches he has been leaning on the bar upon his folded arms, in his characteristic position, regarding the scene sardonically.*)

Chilly: The old joint is getting pretty popular these days.

Vanessa: Oh Chilly, you don't know Miss Simonds, do you?

Ursula: But of course I know you. Everyone knows the famous Chilly Steele. I hope you don't object to me being here?

Chilly: Not much of a place for ladies.

Ursula: But I am not a lady; not in the foolish sense. I would like you to look upon me as a friend, Chilly—a comrade.

Chilly: I've never known any good to come of looking on women as friends, or any other way.

Ursula: I know just what you mean; but in a better organized world order it would be different. I've heard a lot about you. You are in revolt against society. And you are a lone wolf. One-man revolutions are picturesque, but not very practical.

Chilly: I've heard a lot about you, too. You want to be a commie, but they won't have you because they don't trust you. Your Dad left you quite a pile but not enough to buy a Party ticket. But you think they might take you if you could do a little soul-saving for them—getting me to do a few jobs, for instance.

Ursula: I wouldn't think an intelligent man like you would listen to such foolish gossip.

Chilly: What do you want Franz to do? Work up some kind of a Red Punch and Judy?

Vanessa: Chilly, you've been listening at keyholes.

Chilly: No I haven't. Call it second sight if you like. Everybody with an axe to grind wants Franz to grind it for them.

Nicholas: Who are the others?

Chilly: Weir is bringing a couple of them here tonight.

Szabo: Oh yes. The—what did he say—the Recreation Committee, or something like that.

Nicholas: Oh God, not Tapscott?

Chilly: Tapscott and Mattie Philpott.

Vanessa: We'd better go, Ursula.

Ursula: No, I should like to stay, if Chilly doesn't mind.

Chilly: I won't throw you out, but don't break your neck to come back.

Ursula: You are very kind. Can we have some drinks, please?

Chilly: Only soft drinks served.

Ursula: I have heard otherwise.

Chilly: Foolish gossip. Surprised at you for listening.

Ursula: You're a character, Chilly. Somebody should put you in a book.

Chilly: Let 'em catch me, first. My external man—sure, that's easy. Any fool with eyes in his head can describe Chilly Jim. But is that what makes me a character? Nope. It's the soul that makes what we call character. And do you know what the soul is? Of course you don't, but I'm going to tell you. You've seen those Chinese boxes that fit one inside another, so that every box you open contains a new box? The soul is like that, made by the Supreme Chinaman of creation—boxes that diminish until, in the last box of all is the tiny seed that makes me a living thing. Open the boxes and lay 'em aside until personality has gone, and even the disguise that makes me a man instead of a woman is gone, and there will still be a hundred boxes to open. And you talk about putting me in a book! You might fumble a little with the lock of the first box; you might even get a peek under the lid, but what good would it do you? And you talk about putting me in a book, as if I was a sweet pea that could be pressed between the pages!

Ursula: You aren't nearly as complex as you think. You've too much brains to talk that kind of bourgeois nonsense.

Chilly: It's not nonsense. It's the wisdom that a brilliant mind has distilled from a misspent life.

Nicholas: Chilly is a gifted natural theologian.

Vanessa: And we still haven't any drinks.

Chilly: I'll get you some coffee.

(**Edward Weir** *comes in; his expression is that of a man who has had too much elevating conversation.*)

Weir: Who's here tonight, Chilly?

Chilly: You can see 'em all. Why?

Weir: I've got the Moral Element outside in the car, and they won't come in if there are any rowdy characters in the place.

Chilly: Well, let's see: there's Hayward the Educated Second Storey Man, and his moll, Medway. There's the Red Spy Simonds, and Szabo the Moscow Marionette Man. To offset them I can offer Mahatma Buckety Murphy and myself, the Transcendental Honky-Tonk proprietor. How's that?

Nicholas: We'll retire into a corner and pretend we're full of opium if it will help you, Ned. What are they coming for?

Weir: Good works and clean fun, as usual.

(*He goes.* **Nicholas, Vanessa** *and* **Ursula** *move to a table in a corner, where* **Chilly** *takes them cups of coffee.* **Vanessa** *surveys* **Buckety**, *who is asleep and presents an unsatisfactory appearance; after a little thought she removes a flower from her dress and puts it in his hand, so that he appears to be smelling it.* **Ursula** *does not consider this amusing, nor does she join when* **Nicholas** *and* **Vanessa** *pledge each other elaborately in cups of coffee. At this point* **Weir** *returns with* **Orville Tapscott,** *an exuberant, busy man, and* **Mrs. E.C. Philpott,** *who, as a keen advocate of all arts and crafts, wears a great many ornaments in tortured metal and outraged leather; even her spectacles have a hand-made look. Both are a-twitter at finding themselves in* **Chilly's** *den.*)

Tapscott: Well, I must say this doesn't look too bad. I was in a lot tougher looking joints than this when I was school-inspecting up in the north.

Mattie: I suppose the crowd doesn't begin to come till late.

Weir: There is never a crowd here, Mrs. Philpott.

Chilly: Good evening, Mr. Weir. I see you've brought a couple of friends.

Respectable people, I hope?

Weir: Yes, Chilly. I'll be their guarantee.

Chilly: That's good enough. No offence, folks, but a man can't be too careful who comes into his place nowadays. Some awful rowdies around.

Tapscott *(heartily)*: You don't think we look like rowdies, I hope?

Chilly: A fellow never knows. It was your friend who kind of worried me. So much jewellery. Kind of arouses suspicions.

Mattie: But that's craft jewellery. I make it myself.

Chilly: Well, just so long as you come by it respectably.

Mattie: Well really! I think I'm pretty well known in this town.

Chilly: I don't care about that just so long as you don't start anything here. Keep your voice down and go home with the fellow you came with. That's all I ask, and it's little enough.

Tapscott: You're all wrong. This is Mrs. E. C. Philpott, President of the Ladies Craft Culture Club, Women's Convenor of the Hobby Lobby, and Chairwoman of the Crafts Sub-Committee of the Local Recreation Commission. You've heard of Mattie Philpott?

Chilly: Nope.

Tapscott: I'm Tapscott. Never heard of me, either, I suppose?

Chilly: Nope.

Tapscott: Well, it's refreshing to meet with such ignorance. I guess you live completely outside the recreation field.

Chilly: Depends what you mean. Some people consider this the centre of the recreation field.

Mattie: Recreation means "re-creation." What you sell here doesn't create;

it destroys.

Nicholas: May I have another cup of this excellent coffee, Chilly?

Chilly: Right away.

Nicholas: And could I have an egg sandwich, as well? Not too heavy on the condiments, if you please. Good evening, Mrs. Philpott; didn't we meet at the Crystal Craft exhibition last spring?

Mattie: Why, Mr. Hayward! I didn't expect to meet you here.

Nicholas: To tell you the truth, I didn't expect to meet you here, either. You are so busy with your recreation activities that I don't suppose you have much time for enjoyment. But I come here often to look across the water at the city, and enjoy a cup of Chilly's wonderful coffee. May I offer you a cup?

Mattie: Well, to tell you the truth, I had three cups at supper.

Nicholas: A cold fruit juice, then. No no, you mustn't refuse me. And you too, Mr. Tapscott. We haven't met, but I have heard many people speak of you.

Tapscott: Thanks. Very kind, I'm sure.

Nicholas: Chilly, two delicious, vitamin-packed juices. A hop in every drop. What about you, Ned?

Weir: Coffee.

Nicholas: You seem pensive. What's the matter?

Weir *(drawing him aside)*: Don't kid these people, Nick. They may be able to help Szabo.

Nicholas: Fantastic! How?

Weir: Give me a chance.

(**Chilly** *has brought fruit drinks for* **Tapscott** *and* **Mrs. Philpott**; *they are in tall glasses, iced and with tall sprigs of mint in them; they do not look innocent.*

Later he brings coffee for **Nicholas** *and* **Weir**.)

Nicholas: I understand that you are here on business, so I shall return to my table. But I hope that before you go you will be able to meet my friends. Unless you intend to stay very late, of course. *(He goes back to* **Vanessa** *and* **Ursula**.)

Tapscott: Say, this is certainly good juice! Do you sell much of it?

Chilly: Gallons, and gallons, and gallons.

Tapscott: Would you consider selling me the formula? I'd like to put this into the juice bars of every regional recreation centre in the city. This is just what the teenager wants. A juice with a tang!

Mattie: You certainly fix it up nicely. It almost looks wicked. Dainty serving certainly makes a big difference.

Chilly: Thanks. That's the first time anyone ever called me dainty.

Weir: Is Franz around, Chilly?

Chilly: In the kitchen. *(shouts)* Franz!

Szabo *(outside)*: Yes! *(He comes in, still carrying his bit of carving.)*

Weir: This is Franz Szabo. I've told you about him. Franz, Mrs. Philpott and Mr. Tapscott are interested in your work and I want to see if you can be of use to each other.

Szabo: Oh yes. It is very kind of you to come.

Mattie: I still don't understand why you couldn't meet us at the Y.W.C.A.

Weir: That's a long story. The point is, have you any use for a first-class puppet man, and can you help Franz to get on his feet in Canada?

Tapscott: Well, let's be perfectly frank. Let's get right down to work and lay our cards on the table face upwards. Puppets are nothing new here.

Szabo: No. They are not very new anywhere.

Tapscott: Puppets have had a place in the recreational field for years. In fact, at least six puppet groups have been formed right here in our own city. How are they making out, Mrs. Philpott?

Mattie: Well, just at present there isn't much activity; in fact, I think we've pretty well exhausted the puppet. But then, summer is barely over, and we stress outdoor activities in the fine weather. Puppets are only practical in schools, you see.

Szabo: Oh? Why?

Tapscott: Well, puppetry comes under the head of what we call tot-to-teen activities. Simple handicrafts to encourage manual dexterity. After fourteen we figure that the teenager is adjusting to sex and society and he needs group-training and vigorous outdoor sports.

Szabo: But I do not understand. Puppetry is not at all simple. How far did your groups go with their work?

Mattie: Oh, a complete course. Hand puppets—Punch and Judy, you know—then marionettes—the string figures, you understand—and Javanese shadow puppets. It was a very thorough program. Each child had to make at least one puppet.

Szabo: But who taught all this?

Mattie: Miss McConkey of the Collegiate staff; she did a six weeks' summer course in it last year at the College of Education.

Szabo: But Madame, how—? Six weeks?

Mattie: She was really wonderful. She simplified what she had learned for the children, of course. For instance, all the puppets were dressed in long skirts, so that they didn't need any legs, you see. Children find it very hard to make a puppet walk. And the heads were really dolls' heads that she bought in the five-and-ten, to get around all the trouble of modelling. You see, Mr. Szabo, it's no use expecting children to stick to anything that seems difficult. Our recreational courses are worked out on the most modern methods of teaching, and we know that the minute a problem is created, interest wanes.

Szabo: But surely, in games—

Tapscott: Oh, a game is an entirely different proposition.

Szabo: I should say so. Puppets are a very serious matter. I am sure that Miss— Miss what-you-said, is a very charming lady, but in six weeks she could not even get the feel of a single puppet, not to speak of Javanese puppets, and all the puppets in the world. Indeed—I must be frank—women do not make puppet masters. The women of my family made costumes and played the music, but the puppets were handled by the men.

Tapscott: Oh, you'll find it very different here. Puppetry is a girl's project— the sub-teen girl. And scientific teaching speeds up the course.

Szabo: Ach, Gott! And do you want me to teach these little girls to play with dolls that have no legs?

Tapscott: No, no; Miss McConkey has done all that. As a matter of cold fact, the puppet needs a shot in the arm here; as a project the puppet has fallen flat. We want to put the puppet on its feet from a scientific recreational point of view.

Szabo: How can a puppet be on its feet when it has no feet?

Tapscott: Well, what we feel is this. The puppet is a flop as a manual-development project, but there is still a place for the puppet in the social instructional field.

Mattie: Yes, we feel that the puppet has a great future in the tot-lot.

Szabo: Please, what is it, a lot-tot?

Mattie: Tot-lot. It's just what it says—a lot full of tots.

Weir: Franz, a lot is a piece of open ground, and a tot is a child.

Mattie: Not just any child; recreationally speaking, the tot is the three-to-eight age group.

Tapscott: And morons from three to sixteen.

Mattie: Yes, of course. We have to include morons. Now what do you want to get across to the tot?

Szabo: God knows.

Mattie: Socially acceptable behaviour, of course. Now, the question is: how?

Szabo: Ach so; how?

Tapscott *(merrily pretending to blow a trumpet)*: Ta-ta-ta-ta! Enter the puppet!

Mattie: This is Orville's idea, and it appears to me to be one of the greatest strokes of genius in organized recreation!

Tapscott: Here you are, an experienced hand with puppets. You whip up a dozen little plays, based on pamphlets we can give you, and you tour the tot-lots. You set up your little show and you do a ten-minute play, let's say, about a kid who doesn't eat his cereal for breakfast. What happens? He gets sick, and a big dragon called Malnutrition comes to him and says, "Lookit, you've got to eat your cereal." So he does, and when the play ends, he's happy.

Mattie: It helps to assimilate the child to the group, you see. It will revolutionize social training in the tot-lot.

Tapscott: Or take teeth. Kid won't clean his teeth. He goes to bed and dreams he's living in a big white castle that is falling down. Everywhere he goes, things fall apart. Then he discovers he's living in a decayed tooth. He wakes up and says: "I'll always clean my teeth after this. Kids, clean your teeth night and morning and remove particles from between your teeth with dental floss." Curtain.

Szabo: Mr. Tapscott, I—I don't know what to say.

Tapscott: Oh, I understand. This is a big idea and it has to be dealt with in a big way. Mind you, I'm not talking officially now. I'm not even talking on committee level, not to mention executive level. But if you can fix up a few shows, we'll put them on at the inter-regional recreational directors' conference next month, and if they don't throw the meeting into an uproar, well, my name's not Orville Tapscott, that's all.

Mattie: I just can't see it failing, Orville.

Tapscott: Well, Mattie, not everybody in the recreational field has your vision. But mark my words, Szabo, if it goes over, there's no limit to what can follow. Why, the whole audio-visual field opens before us!

Szabo: The—?

Tapscott: Audio-visuals. You know, talking pictures. Or didn't they have them in Europe when you left?

Szabo: Yes, but how can you mix marionettes and talking pictures?

Tapscott: Easily. We film the shows, and exhibit them in schools. Audio-visuals are the coming thing in education. They reduce pupil-resistance by cutting down pupil-effort to the barest minimum. But that's all to come. First we have to win the battle of the tot-lot.

Mattie: You know, Orville, it's masterly. The more you talk about it, the better it sounds.

Tapscott: Thanks, Mat. You know how I feel about your support on this thing. And I've always said that there isn't another woman in the recreational field with your breadth. Well, there's the plan, Szabo. Now let's just kick it around till something comes out of it.

Szabo: Mr. Tapscott, may I say something now?

Tapscott: Go ahead.

Szabo: This plan; it will not do.

Tapscott: Now just a minute. Let's get this straight. The plan is all right. Maybe you won't do. Maybe you haven't the vision. But the plan is all right.

Szabo: No, Mr. Tapscott, the plan is not all right. It is all wrong. It is—what do you say?—cheap and nasty. You say that I should kick it around. Very well, now I shall kick—

Tapscott: Now just a minute. I have had long experience in the recreational field—

Szabo: But I have had longer experience of puppets. I have my own, and my father's, and my grandfather's, back to the time of Shakespeare. I did not learn what I know in six weeks from some other ignoramus. A puppet is a little jointed figure, and I am the puppet master. Yes? But also the puppet is a man, and I am the god who gives him life and a soul—a part of my own soul. I make him so carefully, piece by piece, that I know him better than I know my own body: I do not make him from cheap dolls with no legs. And when I know him, and make him walk and move his arms and dance, I concentrate so hard on him that he is more truly alive than I am myself. He is myself. Now, Mr. Tapscott, tell me: do I use all my skill and inherited tradition and knowledge to make little children eat nasty food or rub their teeth with brushes? Are fifteen generations of puppet masters to end with a harlot of a dirty dog who uses his art to tell nonsense? Don't speak! I know this is the new world and the atomic age, but I know that what has taken three hundred years to make does not lose its value in a few weeks. You are wrong, Mr. Tapscott, and if your nonsense is what your country believes, it is time your country got some sense!

Nicholas: Hear hear!

(The group at the rear table have long since ceased to pretend that they are not listening, and Szabo's speech has electrified them. Nicholas and Vanessa applaud heartily.)

Mattie: Well, after that there doesn't seem much point in staying here. It seems to me that for a man who has only been in this country a short time you express some pretty radical opinions.

Nicholas: What's radical about decency, and honesty, and self respect, and a refusal to cheapen art and drag it in the mud?

Tapscott: Who asked you to butt into this?

Nicholas: Nobody. I just thought that if some plain speaking was being done I'd like to get in on it.

Tapscott: Just oblige me by keeping yourself to yourself, will you? Well,

Weir, this was a wild goose chase, it appears.

Weir: The whole thing is my fault. I thought it might work, but I see now that you and Szabo could never agree. I'm sorry to have wasted everybody's time.

Szabo: No, Mr. Weir, you are my friend.)
)
Tapscott: No, Ned, relations between the) *(speaking together)*
paper and the recreation authorities must)
not be affected by this.)

Weir: Please! I apologise to everybody! Is that all right?

Vanessa: Oh Ned, you poor darling, everyone has hurt your feelings!

Tapscott: No; the best plan is forget the whole thing. Now, Mrs. Philpott and I both have a meeting at the Y at nine, and we'll have to go now if we are to be on time. As for you, Szabo, it'll take you five years to become a citizen, and I hope that by that time you'll have learned that in this country art is proud and happy to consider itself the handmaid of education.

Szabo: I shall always believe that education is something which helps men to appreciate art.

Tapscott: Come on, Mattie.

Chilly: Just a minute. Before you go I've got a word of advice for you two. You mix too much with kids. And do you know what happens to people who mix too much with kids? They get ringworm!

(Exeunt **Mrs. Philpott** *and* **Tapscott.***)*

Weir: Look, I'm terribly sorry! I didn't know they would be like that!

Nicholas: Forget about it, Ned. Send them away to the Y, and come back. We all love you, though your sins be as scarlet.

Weir: Oh well— *(He goes.)*

Chilly: I guess that calls for a drink all round.

Ursula: Didn't you tell me you weren't a bootlegger?

Chilly *(with dignity)*: I deny the allegation and I defy the allegator. If I give you a drink in my place of residence, that makes you my guest, though in your case, Miss Simonds, it fails to make you my friend.

(At the magical word "drink" **Buckety** *has wakened; he regards his flower with bewildered disgust, then throws it away and makes one of his swooping descents upon the room.)*

Buckety: Have I been missing anything?

Nicholas: You have missed a very remarkable defeat of the powers of uplift by the powers of common sense, a great rarity in our fair land, Buckety. Unfortunately it leaves our friend Franz exactly where he was.

Szabo: But you know, I cannot understand this at all. I talk very largely about art; really, I never thought about my marionettes as art before I came to this country. I just thought of them as entertainment. It was all simple. Why can't it be simple here?

Ursula: Nothing can be simple in a world revolution. An economic system is crumbling, a class system is crumbling, and the old world is in travail to bring forth the new. And you ask for simplicity!

Buckety: Right, lady! It's a changing world, and if you don't change you get left, eh?

Ursula: Exactly. Who are you?

Buckety: I'm the suffering proletariat!

Vanessa: He's Buckety Murphy, Ursula.

Buckety: Ursula? Are you Ursula Simonds, the rich commie?

Ursula: I am not rich and I will not be called a commie.

Buckety: Yes you are. You're stinking rich. I've heard about you.

Nicholas: Go away, Buckety. I disagree completely with you, Miss Simonds. All this talk about dying old worlds and wonderful new ones is stupid and misleading. Revolutions never change anything that matters; they merely put power in new hands, and the new masters have to serve their apprenticeship to civilization, like the rulers they have overthrown.

(A car is heard starting outside, and during the next speeches **Weir** *enters.)*

Ursula: I would have expected you to have more faith in progress, Mr. Hayward.

Nicholas: There is no such thing as progress; there is only change. The highest in life is always there for those who want it, but not many of us want it. The only revolutions that make any real difference to the world are revolutions in the hearts of individual men.

Ursula: That sounds suspiciously like Christianity.

Nicholas: Yes, doesn't it? But what I have said was already old before Christ was dreamed of.

Buckety: Listen. Lemme speak—

Weir: Franz, I didn't blame you for what you said to Tapscott, but you must realize that in his horrible way he is a man of some power. Now, I've persuaded him to take a look at a puppet show along your lines, and if he likes it, he might get you something to do in connection with the public library system.

Szabo: You are too kind to me, Mr. Weir. I have a bad tongue. When does Mr. Tapscott want to see me again?

Weir: A week from tonight. Can you have a play ready?

Szabo: A play! A week! Impossible!

Weir: Oh, stop saying impossible! Can't you learn anything about compromise?

Nicholas: You must make a try, Franz. We'll help you all we can.

Vanessa: Yes, we'll do anything you say.

Szabo: Very well. I'll do my best. No—not my best; I'll do whatever can be done in a week.

Weir: That's the spirit!

Buckety: Listen! Miss Simonds, listen to me!

Ursula: Oh, what is it?

Buckety *(urgently)*: Lookit, do you know what's wrong with you? Do you know what's behind this communism of yours? I seen a dozen cases like yours. Hundreds of 'em. You need a man, that's what!

Ursula: Don't you dare speak to me in that way!

Buckety: It's for your own good. And I've got just the fellow for you. Great experience of life and a wonderful physique. Lookit! Take a look at these cards! "The Toilet of Hercules." Look at them muscles. They're yours for the taking. And all I ask is marriage. The plain gold band. Is it a deal? Come on, Urs! Is it a deal?

*(***Ursula*** *has shrunk from him and he now follows her urgently.)*

Ursula: Get away from me, you filthy scum!

(During the foregoing, **Chilly** *has hauled his booze bucket out of the water, having prepared glasses for drinks all round. Now, with calm decision, he douses* **Buckety** *with a pailful of cold water.)*

Chilly: Cut that out, Buck. I won't have any of that here. That's what gets a place a bad name.

Buckety: Dirty, bloody swine! Won't treat a man like a human being. Ain't I human? Ain't I one of God's creatures?

Ursula: Isn't there a man here with the decency to take me home?

Buckety: Life's a cheat, I tell you! A dirty, bloody, lousy cheat!

(But nobody pays any attention to either of the outraged parties: **Nicholas** *and* **Vanessa** *are deep in conversation,* **Weir** *is consulting a pocket calendar, and* **Szabo** *has resumed work on his puppet, at a brisker pace than before;* **Chilly,** *calm as ever, is mopping his floor.)*

(Curtain)

Act Three

(It is a week later. Upon the bar stands a pretty, bravely painted little marionette stage. The concealment for the puppeteers is not so fine, and consists of a few frowsy curtains. [N.B. These should be arranged so that, if necessary, a skilled puppeteer can be concealed behind them without the knowledge of the audience.] It is night, and the room is warmly, but not brightly, lit, and moonlight falls upon the water and the city in the distance.

When the curtain rises, **Vanessa, Nicholas, Weir, Chilly** *and* **Buckety** *are standing about the stage, looking with satisfaction upon their creation. When* **Weir** *speaks his voice betrays his deep excitement.)*

Weir: Well, is that everything?

*(***Szabo*** *pops his head over the top of the concealing curtains and smiles.)*

Szabo: Everything that we can do for the present, I think.

Weir: Nothing to do now but wait.

Vanessa: I wish we had something better to wait for. Tapscott and Philpott don't deserve this. It's like getting excited and preparing a wonderful party, and realizing at the last minute that the guests aren't really up to it.

Szabo: It is only a beginning; there will be better guests later, we hope.

Vanessa: I suppose so, but I like things to happen quickly and be done with; then I can go on to something else. I hate being tied to things.

Weir: I wish I weren't so nervous.

Szabo: Please do not worry. You will do well.

Nicholas: It looks wonderfully festive, doesn't it?

Chilly: I never expected to see anything like that in this joint. It gives me a feeling I haven't had since I was a kid—a religious feeling.

Vanessa: Religious? Why, Chilly!

Chilly: Yes, religious. You know how religion is: you've always suspected that something existed, and you've wished and prayed that it did exist, and in your dreams you've seen little bits of it, but to save your life you couldn't describe it or put a name to it. Then, all of a sudden, there it is, and you feel grateful, and humble, and wonder how you ever doubted it. That little stage makes me feel like that—quiet and excited at the same time.

Vanessa: Fantastic.

Nicholas: No. I see exactly what Chilly means. I feel much the same myself. It fills a need in the heart. Why not call the feeling it arouses religious? Look at it: brilliant colour, warmth and gaiety—qualities men once sought in the churches, and seek in vain, now. Even our theatres are too self-conscious for gilt and crimson; yet many of us crave these things, deep in our hearts.

Weir: You really think that many do?

Nicholas: I am sure of it.

Weir: Enough to keep Franz going, I hope.

Buckety (*comes down between* **Vanessa** *and* **Chilly**): Ah, now there you touch on an important point. As I see it, the big thing is to keep Franz's show from getting clicky. That's the trouble with too many things; a click gets hold of it, and sucks the juice out of it, and kills it. We've got to keep this thing out of the hands of a click. That's why I'm afraid of this Tapscott thing; that fellow's in a kind of a do-good click that'd kill anything.

Nicholas: But Buck, we've got to get Franz started somehow. He has no money. If Tapscott can get him work with a few big libraries, it will put him on his feet.

Buckety: Libraries! Clicks!

Chilly: Listen here, Bucket o' Slops, you keep out of sight when Tapscott comes, or he'll think this show is in the hands of a click of seedy goofguzzlers. D'you hear?

Buckety: Sure, Chilly. You may rely on my discretion. *(He moves round back to puppet show.)*

Chilly: You can rely on the toe of my boot if you don't watch yourself. *(He begins to move tables to R. back.)*

Weir: Nearly half-past eight. I'll have to go for Tapscott and Mrs. Philpott. Now, is there anything still to be done?

Nicholas: No. Don't fuss, Ned.

Weir: I won't be long. They're just over at the City Hall, and I promised to pick them up.

Vanessa: Oh Ned, would you be wonderful and pick up Ursula Simonds at the same time.

Weir: What for?

Vanessa: Why do you suppose? She wants to come.

Weir: But Vanessa, this is awfully important to Franz, and Mattie Philpott hates Ursula. A great many people do. Couldn't she come some other time?

Vanessa: I promised her that she could come.

Nicholas: I don't think that you should have done that.

Vanessa: I suppose you are one of those who don't like her.

Nicholas: Yes, I am; but that's not the point. She may queer things for Szabo.

Vanessa: I'm sorry, but I've asked her, and I promised that someone would call for her, in case she has any more trouble with your friend Buckety. Don't forget that I have done a good deal of work for tonight's demonstration, too. Why should you men do all the inviting?

Weir: I must go. I'll bring her, Vanessa, but I wish she didn't have to ride in my car with Mattie Philpott. (**Weir** *goes.*)

Vanessa: Men are terribly high-strung creatures. What a fuss you are all making—even Chilly.

Chilly: Why shouldn't I be high-strung? Let me tell you a useful secret: when you want to know what a man is, imagine the exact opposite of what he seems; that'll give you the key of his character. Remember what I said, Buckety.

Buckety: You haven't a thing to worry about from me; just watch out for them clicks.

(**Chilly** *retires to the kitchen, and* **Buckety** *goes to his accustomed haunt by the river.* **Vanessa** *climbs a step-ladder by the bar to re-drape the masking curtains.*)

Vanessa *(her back to* **Nicholas***)*: Don't sulk, Nicky. Ursula won't eat you.

Nicholas: I can't understand what you want with her.

Vanessa: Oh, I quite like her. You mustn't be jealous of my friends.

Nicholas: I'm not jealous. Or perhaps I am. Why is it that I have less influence with you than somebody like Ursula? Any of your acquaintances seem to carry more weight with you than I do.

Vanessa: Why should you have influence with me, Nicky?

Nicholas: You know why.

Vanessa: But I want you to say it.

Nicholas: Because I love you.

Vanessa *(turns to him)*: Dear Nicky.

Nicholas: I wish you meant that. But I don't think I am very dear to you. There have been times when I have been almost sure you loved me, but you have never said so.

Vanessa: Yes, there have been times when I was almost sure, but it wouldn't be fair to say so unless I were really sure, would it? Have I been ungenerous to you, Nicky?

Nicholas: The smallest favour from you is so much to me that I couldn't estimate its value, and say whether you have been generous or not. If you had any idea how much I love you, you couldn't talk of generosity, for that implies giving a part of what one has. I ask you to take all that I am, and all that I ever shall be, and to give me your love in return.

Vanessa: And if I can't?

Nicholas: Then I must take less, if you cannot give me all.

Vanessa: And if I cannot give anything?

Nicholas: You have given more than you think already, and if you were to leave me tonight you could not take it from me.

Vanessa: Your love frightens me a little bit, Nicky. It is so constant. What I feel for you changes from day to day and sometimes from hour to hour. Have you never thought that if I were a little less certain of you I might fall in love with you?

Nicholas: I don't want to play a cat and mouse game with you, and I don't understand what you mean by falling in love. You once said that you knew I loved you before I told you so. If that were true, did it never occur to you to look at your own feeling for me? I don't believe that you thought I would simply be an interesting scalp to hang at your belt.

Vanessa: Nicky dear, men mustn't complain about the way women treat them; it makes them look foolish.

Nicholas: I'm sorry if I look foolish to you; but I don't think I look foolish to anyone else. I love you, and when I say that, I am not playing with words.

Vanessa: But I think that you get quite a bit of satisfaction from the role of slighted swain.

Nicholas: A man whose trade is understanding literature is apt to become a connoisseur of his own feelings, but I am more sincere in this than I have ever been.

Vanessa: You're a dear boy, but frightfully serious.

Nicholas: Yes, frightfully serious, but I am not a boy. I am thirty-five, and if I am ever to be a man I am a man now. You can analyse what I feel for you, and discover discreditable explanations for it in psychology, I suppose, but it is the strongest and best feeling I have ever had, and I am not ashamed of it.

Vanessa: I'm sorry if I was flippant about it, Nicholas. But I just don't know how to cope.

Nicholas: I wish I knew how to cope, myself. But so much longing and remorse and fear and happiness is more than I can control. I must have some hint from you about what is likely to happen.

Vanessa: How do you mean?

Nicholas: I've told you that I am not a boy. For a boy, being in love is enough in itself, but for a man it is not.

Vanessa: We've talked about marriage.

Nicholas: Yes, but of course you couldn't make up your mind.

Vanessa: You're ten years older than I; perhaps I am not ready for certainties.

Nicholas: How old will I be when you are?

Vanessa: It depends on so many things.

Nicholas: Only because you cannot make up your mind about one thing.

Vanessa: Oh Nicky, do you think that I can love you simply by making up my mind that I will? Don't be such a fool. You're asking for certainties— very high-flown certainties. You want the future all cut-and-dried, on the highest level. Don't you suppose I would like a peep into the future? When I am your age and you are middle-aged, how will life look then?

Nicholas: I'm doing my best to make sure that it will be attractive.

Vanessa: I know. The job in the States. But you really hate the idea, don't you?

Nicholas: You know what I think. If I have to leave my own country to find a market for my talents—a fair market—I will do it, as thousands of others have done it. But I won't pretend to like it.

Vanessa: Nor would you ever forgive me for making you do it.

Nicholas: It isn't a simple decision about money; it's really a decision about what century one wants to live in. The things that concern me—scholarship and the arts—still linger in the nineteenth century in Canada; we still pretend to be pioneers, for whom such things are luxuries, and not necessities. I've made up my mind to go to the States because I want a better job, more money, and generous recognition if I deserve it. Canadians hate you so for being one of themselves. But I think of it chiefly as a flight in time—a leap from the nineteenth century into the twentieth.

Vanessa: But you would rather stay, and try to regulate the clock, wouldn't you? You love Canada.

Nicholas: I wouldn't say so. Whenever I hear a Canadian say that he loves this country, I suspect him of being a neurotic or a rascal. This is not yet the kind of country a man loves; it is a country that he respects and worries about. The mainspring of a Canadian's patriotism is not love, but duty.

Vanessa: And duty demands that you stay here.

Nicholas: Yes, but love—love for you, and love for many, many things that make life sweet for me—drives me elsewhere.

Vanessa: You take it very hardly, don't you. Not many people would.

Nicholas: I am what I am. I must do what my nature makes me do.

Vanessa: Nicky dear, I have to make an awfully difficult decision. I don't love you: sometimes I almost do, but that's not the same. You love me, and I suppose that gives you a claim on me, though I've never really understood why. You must have noticed how little attention poets and novelists give to the predicament of the person who is loved, and who does not love in return. If we marry and go south you will always feel, in your heart's core, that I made you shirk your duty; if I never grow to love you, that will be a tragedy. I don't have to tell you what tragedy is: you have told too many classes that Sir Philip Sidney says, "Tragedy concerneth a high fellow." You are a high fellow, Nicky, and your ruin would be a tragedy. So I think we'd better part.

Nicholas: No!

Vanessa: Yes, Nicky.

Nicholas: But am I to have nothing to say whatever?

Vanessa: I daren't let you say anything; you are too persuasive. Dear Nicky, I hope that there will never be a time when you think that I used a high-sounding patriotic quibble to get out of a difficult place. You know what sort of person I am—very fond of my own way, impatient, quickly tired of things and people, but I am honest. You think I am cruel to talk like this, but the real cruelty would be to accept your love without giving all of my own. I know that this hurts now, but if I took the weak course and married you, that would be the death-blow of everything that is best in you.

(A car is heard approaching, and there are voices outside.)

Nicholas: You can't expect me to accept that. I—

Vanessa: No; think it over, Nicky, before you protest.

(Weir *enters from outside, showing in* **Mrs. Philpott, Ursula Simonds** *and* **Tapscott.)**

Weir: Where are the others?

Vanessa: I'll call them. *(She goes to the kitchen, removing the step-ladder.)*

Mattie: Good evening, Mr. Hayward. You seem to be here a great deal.

Nicholas: I might say the same of you, Mrs. Philpott. I hope you are well?

Tapscott: You've got the stage all fixed up, I see. Looks nice. For a child audience, though, maybe you want more of the Disney touch. Some bunnies climbing around on that curtain would look good.

(**Chilly** *has come in with a couple of kerosene lamps which he places behind reflectors, so that they appear to throw a warm light on the puppet stage.*)

Chilly: Why bunnies?

Tapscott: Oh, kind of symbol of childhood, I guess. You always put bunnies on everything for children. Bunnies or cookies.

(**Chilly** *looks at* **Tapscott** *and his lips move in an unmistakably profane manner, though no words can be distinguished.*)

Mattie: That's really a very nice piece of project-work. *(She approaches the little stage.)*

Chilly: Don't touch it.

Mattie: Why not?

Chilly: For decency's sake, that's why not. When you go to church you don't expect to play the organ, do you? Haven't you any sense of mystery, woman?

Tapscott: Look here, you, Mrs. Philpott is a handicrafts expert.

Chilly: Look here, you, this is the theatre, and if you get too fresh with it, you kill it.

Nicholas *(pouring oil)*: These chairs will give you an excellent view. I'm sure Franz will be anxious to show you everything afterward.

(**Weir** *and* **Vanessa** *return; he goes to the* **Philpott-Tapscott** *group, she to* **Ursula**, *who has remained at a distance.*)

Vanessa: Hello, Ursula; did you have any trouble on the way?

Ursula: No; everything was quite peaceful. When does the play begin?

Vanessa: Now.

Weir: We're ready. There's just one thing I want to explain. Szabo has no expert helper, and I'm doing what I can. I'm terrible, really. So if anything goes wrong, it's my fault, you see.

Nicholas: None of the rest of us could do anything with the puppets at all.

Weir: I feel as if I might be sick.

Nicholas: You haven't time. Away you go. (**Weir** *goes miserably behind the curtains.*)

Vanessa: Come on, Ursula; we'll sit here.

Nicholas: Ladies and gentlemen, may I say a few words of introduction? It was out of the question to get up a complete puppet play in a week, and what you are going to see is merely a fragment—a demonstration of what Franz Szabo can do. It is a short scene from one of his most successful puppet plays, "Don Quixote"—the scene in which the knight charges against the windmills. This is a good scene for the purpose, because it requires only three characters: Don Quixote, his horse Rosinante, and his servant Sancho Panza. *(Here he is prodded in the back from behind the curtains.)* All right Ned, all right. Mr. Weir wishes me to state that he is utterly incompetent to assist in this performance, and invites you to guess which puppet he is controlling.

Weir *(thrusting his head through the curtains)*: Listen, I'm Sancho Panza, and you mustn't hold what I do against Franz—

Nicholas: Get back, Ned! You're being extremely unprofessional!

Weir: Yes, but I want to make it clear—*(Unseen hands drag him out of sight.)*

Nicholas: Stage fright. It will be kinder to pretend that we didn't see him. One more word. I shall read the lines the puppets are supposed to speak; it isn't usual, but Franz is nervous about his English, and Ned can't memorize anything. Can we have the lights out, Chilly? And now, the overture.

(**Chilly** *turns out the lights which do not illuminate the stage, so that the audience is in half-darkness.* **Nicholas** *plays a short piece on the gramophone which sits on the bar. During the music* **Idris Rowlands**, *rather drunk, enters from outside and seats himself apart from the others, who do not notice him.*

Buckety *alone sees him come in, for he has been sneaking forward to see the puppet show; he sits at* **Rowlands'** *feet.*

> *The curtains of the puppet stage part; the scene is a plain, painted in sharp perspective; several windmills are seen in the distance, and on the stage there is one windmill with sails which may be made to revolve. The puppet of Don Quixote enters, walking.)*

Don Quixote (Nicholas *speaks)*: Noble knights and gentle ladies, I greet you! Know that I am a knight of Spain, deeply read in books of chivalry; I roam the world as you see me, in armour and helmet, bearing my trusty lance, and striking blows wherever I may in defence of truth and right. And all to do honour to the fairest of damsels, my exquisite mistress, the lovely Dulcinea.

Tapscott: Not bad, not bad. Some pretty hard words in it for kids, though. And what's all this about a mistress?

Don Quixote *(in* **Szabo**'*s voice)*: Please, my lord Tapscott, do not misunderstand. My mistress is a lady whose virtue I defend. Now your mistress, if you have one, is a lady whose virtue you take away.

Tapscott: That's enough of that! I'm on the board of the Y.

Don Quixote (Szabo): That is what I mean. A knight and a member of the board of the Y use the word in different senses.

Tapscott: That'll do! Get on with the show.

Don Quixote (Nicholas): My companion in my wanderings is my faithful squire, Sancho Panza, and here he comes.

(The puppet of **Sancho** *is dragged on the stage;* **Weir**'*s voice is heard muttering nervously, and* **Szabo** *is heard reassuring him.)*

Sancho (Nicholas): Master, the life of a wandering knight may be glorious to you, but to me it seems poor enough. What have we had from it yet but blows, hard words, and misfortune? Life at home was better.

Don Quixote (Nicholas): Nay, my faithful companion, life seems poor to you because you look at it through the eyes of a peasant. But I shall make you a gentleman and my esquire, and then you shall perceive the glories of knight-errantry and high adventure. Kneel. *(The puppet of Sancho kneels, or rather, subsides clumsily upon the ground.)*

Sancho: How will kneeling help me?

Don Quixote: Now, Sancho, I declare you to be my squire and true companion, and my servant no more. Arise, Squire Sancho.

Sancho: What, am I a gentleman now?

Don Quixote: A gentleman and an esquire.

Sancho: And is my old woman a lady? She, who knows nothing but how to wash the clothes and scrub the stones?

Tapscott: We'll have to have that out.

Mattie: Yes, that would never do; it would just create class feeling among the children.

Tapscott: Anyway, it's against a high ideal of womanhood. Still, this is just a rough idea for a show, anyway. Go on.

Don Quixote: And now, Squire Sancho, bring me my trusty steed Rosinante, for I must seek some glorious adventure in which I may uphold the matchless beauty and virtue of my lady, the fair Dulcinea.

Sancho: Does your worship mean Rosinante, the old skeleton, the old bonebag? Why, sir, she is not good for anything but to be sold to make glue, or soup for paupers.

Mattie: I don't think that will do. First the poor woman, and now the poor horse. After all, if we can't have a play without making fun of others, it's a poor lookout, isn't it?

Don Quixote: Squire Sancho, I desire you to bring hither that matchless courser, that peerless Arabian steed, the swift-footed Rosinante.

Sancho: As your worship pleases. *(The puppet of Sancho is dragged ignominiously off the stage.)*

Don Quixote: O Dulcinea, most glorious of created beings, accept, I beg, the exploits of my arms as tribute to your beauty.

Tapscott: I haven't got this figured out, yet. Who is this Dulcy, or whatever her name is, that he keeps talking about?

Nicholas: That is his mist—the lady he loves.

Tapscott: Well, is he going to fight somebody for her, or something?

Nicholas: Yes. Don't you understand? He performs deeds of great daring to do honour to his lady-love.

Tapscott: I don't get that, at all. She isn't around to see him fight.

Mattie: No, that's not clear to me, either.

Rowlands: That's not the only thing that isn't clear to you.

Tapscott *(peering into the darkness)*: Who said that?

Vanessa: Oh hello, Professor Rowlands.

Tapscott: What do you mean by insulting Mrs. Philpott?

Rowlands: What is that to you? Is she your Dulcinea, by any chance?

Mattie: Pay no attention, Orville. The man is obviously drunk.

Rowlands: You're damned right I'm drunk.

Chilly: Listen, Professor; take it easy.

Rowlands *(rises and bows)*: I beg your pardon. I am extremely sorry if I have been making myself objectionable.

Nicholas: May we go on, now?

Tapscott: Just a minute. There are one or two things I want to get ironed out. Who is this Dulcy?

Nicholas: Dulcinea is the lady Don Quixote loves.

Tapscott: Oh, she's the heroine?

Nicholas: No, she is old and ugly.

Tapscott: Well, what's the sense of that?

Nicholas: It would take rather a long time to explain. It is a satire, you see.

Tapscott: No, I don't see at all. Anyway, satire is no good for children—not even for teenagers.

Rowlands: Excuse me, sir; are you entirely unacquainted with the story of Don Quixote?

Tapscott: Certainly not. I did it at the university.

Rowlands: Read it, you mean?

Tapscott: No. It was on a general literature course. You're a professor; you ought to know that if we read all the stuff on those courses we'd have no time for extra-mural activities.

Rowlands: I see. You did not go to the university to learn?

Tapscott: I learned enough for my degree, but you know as well as I do that the important thing in university life is rubbing up against other people.

Rowlands: I do not know when I have heard a dubious theory of education more indelicately expressed.

Nicholas: Shall we go on with the play? We can have a discussion afterward.

Chilly: Professor, for God's sake pipe down, will you?

Nicholas: Let's get on with it, Franz.

(The puppet of **Sancho Panza** *re-enters, leading* **Rosinante,** *a broken-down miserable nag.)*

Sancho: Here she is, your worship, and hardly able to stand. Gee up, there, Rosinante! *(The horse collapses to the floor.)*

Don Quixote: Incomparable courser, how she paws the ground! Her eyes flash fire! Her nostrils breathe defiance to the world! Oh worthy steed of a worthy knight! *(The horse suddenly leaps up and snorts.)*

Don Quixote: Aha, she scents some worthy exploit! *(The sails of the windmill begin to turn.)*

Don Quixote: What is it, my charger? What, yonder? See, Pancho, see! An army of giants approaches across the plain!

Sancho: Nay master, they are windmills!

Don Quixote: Giants! Giants! See, the foremost of them all challenges me to mortal combat! Look how he waves his four arms in defiance. But had he as many arms as Briareus, I am for him! To horse! To horse! To horse!

*(With difficulty, **Don Quixote** mounts **Rosinante**, who collapses a couple of times; but at last he is secure, and rides offstage on the side opposite to the windmill.)*

Sancho: Oh, my poor master! Alas, the poor mad gentleman! So touched in his wits that he cannot tell a windmill from a giant!

Don Quixote *(offstage)*: For honour, chivalry, and the Lady Dulcinea!

*(There is a tremendous clatter of horse's hooves, growing louder and louder, until the **Don**, mounted on **Rosinante**, comes upon the stage at quite a slow pace; he rushes at the windmill, seems to fix a lance in one of the sails, is lifted into the air high out of sight, and then he and **Rosinante** fall upon the stage with a clatter. The curtains of the puppet show close. The others applaud, but **Mattie** leaps to her feet.)*

Mattie: Wait! Did I understand you to say that the old man is mad?

Nicholas: Mad as a hatter, Mrs. Philpott.

Mattie: Oh, but that won't do, you know.

Nicholas: It has done extremely well for three centuries.

Mattie: Oh, but we have psychology today, you know. We can't show a play to children which has a maladjusted person as the chief character.

Nicholas: But Don Quixote is one of the great characters of the world's literature.

Tapscott: No, Mrs. Philpott is right. You teach kids to make fun of a lunatic and first thing you know they'll all be delinquents.

Rowlands: Or the first thing you know they'll be making fun of fatheads like you.

Tapscott: You mind your own business, will you?

Rowlands: This is my business. Nothing that concerns humanity is alien to me. Everything is my business.

(During the ensuing scene everyone talks, and the hubbub increases as tension mounts, though only the following lines are clearly heard.)

Mattie: We've got to protect the child against such brutal stories as this! That poor horse! We must teach them to love dumb animals.

Vanessa: Nobody was hurting Rosinante; she was quite happy!

Nicholas: Please! I think you have misunderstood our intention!

Mattie: We can't throw overboard thirty years of child psychology!

Nicholas: And we can't throw overboard a three-hundred-years-old classic.

Vanessa: I think you and Mr. Tapscott are taking a very stuffy attitude toward this whole thing!

Mattie: Miss Medway, I don't know what your connection is with this affair, but I must ask you not to interfere!

Vanessa: I helped make the puppet show, and I think it's good!

Tapscott: It's not good by our standards, and we judge both as educationists and recreation experts.

Nicholas: Oh, recreation be damned!

Mattie: You be careful of your language, Mr. Hayward.

Ursula: You're all wrong, the whole pack of you! The play is no good because it has no message! Give it meaning! Make Sancho the proletariat; make Don Quixote class government; make the windmills capitalism and private profit! Then you will have a play that makes sense!

Nicholas: Then you'll have a chunk of propaganda!

Ursula: Anything with a meaning is propaganda to you. Bourgeois! You only trust art when it is meaningless!

Nicholas: I only trust art in the hands of artists!

Ursula: Bah! Tame cat! University gelding!

Tapscott: Now listen here! This play will have to be changed a lot and cleaned up, or so far as I'm concerned it will never get inside a public library. I want to help, but there are principles of recreational psychology and creative character-building that have to be observed.

Rowlands *(advancing, and brandishing his stick)*: Fools! Fools! Asses! Dolts! Boobies! Muckworms! Dogsbodies! Maggots! Nameless bastards of dishonoured she-apes! Out of my sight before I vomit! *(He pulls down the puppet show with his stick;* **Chilly** *and* **Nicholas** *seize the lamps, and as they dodge to avoid his blows the light sweeps confusedly about the stage.)* Down, down, down, down! Ruin before dishonour! Better death than rape! *(He now turns upon* **Mattie** *and* **Tapscott,** *and as their protests and the cries of the others add to the confusion he drives them to the door.)* Get out, you sneaking, mealy-mouthed obscenities! You Nice Nellies! Go, you donkeys in the temple of art! Be ye forever accursed! Anathema! Anathema!! Anathema!!! *(Striking and thrusting, he drives them to the door and out into the night. He stands for a moment in triumph, then seems to collapse, and* **Chilly** *and* **Nicholas** *gently lead him to a chair.)*

Rowlands: Nicholas! Nicholas!

Nicholas: I'm right here, Idris. Don't break down, old man; you did the only possible thing. Get him a drink, Chilly.

Rowlands: No, I don't want a drink. Had too much already.

Nicholas: I know, I know.

Rowlands: But that wasn't why I did it. I was sober as a judge. I was a judge. I judged them, and found them wanting. I drove them forth, because they were unworthy. And I destroyed the temple because I could not bear to see it profaned.

Szabo *(has watched all of this from the ruins of the show on top of the bar, but now he leaps down)*: You were right, Professor Rowlands. You did what I wished to do myself.

Rowlands: Poor Szabo. I've queered everything for you.

Szabo: Oh no; not everything.

Rowlands: But that's Canada, Szabo. That's what it will do to your puppets and to you. It will freeze your heart with folly and ignorance.

Szabo: No, Professor, I do not think it will. I am an artist, you know, and a real artist is very, very tough. This is my country now, and I am not afraid of it. There may be some bad times; there may be some misunderstandings. But I shall be all right. So long as I keep the image of my work clear in my heart, I shall not fail. The educated like my work, and the uneducated like it. As for the half-educated—well, we can only pray for them in Canada, as elsewhere. Mr. Hayward and Mr. Weir feel badly; they are not used to showing what is precious to them to people who do not understand it or want it; we artists learn very young not to mind too much. We must be tough, and hopeful, too. See, out of the wreck I have Don Quichotte; he met the windmills and he is safe.

Ursula: It is the tough, hopeful men who will build the future.

Szabo: Thank you, Madame. And though I know you do not like to think so,

I believe they will build it a little haphazard.

Weir: Good old Franz; you met the windmills, and you are safe.

Nicholas: I suppose we should do something about this mess.

Weir: I have a terrible feeling, which I can only attribute to a very good upbringing, that I should go out and try to find Tapscott and Mrs. Philpott. They have probably fallen into the river by this time.

Chilly: Will there be anything about this in the *True Briton,* Ned?

Weir: Probably not. One of the enduring regrets of newspapermen is that brawls like this one can only be reported if they end up in police court. But the best brawls involve the best people, and the best people hate to appear in court. Philpott and Tapscott will huff and puff, but they won't lay charges. The best people prefer to be disorderly in private. I fear that this evening's doings are destined to become legend, rather than police court news.

Ursula: If you are going back to town, may I ride with you?

Weir: Yes, but when we find the outraged recreationists you must promise me not to say anything unkind to them. I shall do my best to soothe them.

Nicholas: Can it be done?

Weir: I'm an old hand at soothing. And they're not bad souls, really. They have a simple belief in their own power to do good.

Chilly *(who has brought coffee to* **Rowlands**): Well, I hate simple people, with their simple beliefs. A simple belief in the multiplication tables don't make you a mathematician; a simple belief in God don't make you a saint; and a simple belief in your power to do good don't make you fit to boss everybody and give them lip. To hell with simplicity, I say!

Vanessa: I'll come with you, Ned, and help look for the lost sheep.

Weir: Let's go, then. The longer we wait the harder it will be to smooth them down.

(He and **Ursula** *go;* **Chilly** *is sweeping;* **Buckety** *has removed the gramophone to the kitchen, and* **Szabo** *is methodically sorting the rubbish of his theatre.)*

Szabo: Miss Medway, would you like to take the little curtains? You made them.

Vanessa: No, Franz; you keep them to remember me by.

Szabo: I shall. You have been most kind.

Nicholas: Vanessa.

Vanessa: What is it, Nicky?

Nicholas: I've decided that you are right.

Vanessa: About—?

Nicholas: Yes.

Vanessa: Then we shan't be seeing one another, I suppose?

Nicholas: Oh yes. But perhaps not for some time.

Vanessa: Goodbye, dear Nicholas. *(She kisses him lightly, and goes.)*

Rowlands *(who has neither seen nor heard, sings softly to himself)*:
> Fortune, my foe,
> Why dost thou frown on me?
> And will thy favours
> Never greater be?
> Frown though ye may,
> Yet shall you smile again;
> Nor shall my days
> Pass all in grieving pain.

Buckety *(returning)*: Mr. Hayward.

Nicholas: Mm?

Buckety: Those old jokes you collect: I got a beauty for you. Real old. My father always loved it. D'you know what Noah said to Mrs. Noah when he heard the rain on the roof? (**Nicholas** *shakes his head.*) "Ark!"

Nicholas: Too late, I'm afraid, Buckety. The joke's over.

Buckety: Eh?

Nicholas: I don't know whether I'll write that book or not. I won't do it for some time, anyhow. There's no hurry.

Buckety: What about going to the States?

Nicholas: I think I'll stay here instead.

Szabo: Nicholas! What's changed you?

Nicholas: I don't think I could tell you. Perhaps I don't know completely myself. You are partly responsible.

Szabo: I?

Nicholas: Yes. If you can stay in Canada, I can, too. Everybody says Canada is a hard country to govern, but nobody mentions that for some people it is also a hard country to live in. Still, if we all run away it will never be any better. So let the geniuses of easy virtue go southward; I know what they feel too well to blame them. But for some of us there is no choice; let Canada do what she will with us, we must stay.

Rowlands: Perhaps you'll succeed where I have failed.

Nicholas: Perhaps so. Perhaps not.

Rowlands (*wrapped up in his concerns, sings again*)**:**
> Fortune, my foe,
> Why dost thou frown on me?
> And will thy favours
> Never greater be?

Szabo (*speaking through the song*)**:** Perhaps, some day, we shall learn that the giants were only windmills after all.

Rowlands *(singing)*:
> Frown though ye may,
> Yet shall you smile again;
> Nor shall my days
> Pass all in grieving pain.

(The fall of the curtain coincides with the end of the song. **Buckety** *is eating the sugar out of* **Rowlands'** *coffee cup;* **Chilly** *is leaning on the bar, as usual;* **Nicholas** *picks up the curtains of the puppet theatre and passes his hand gently over them. All are deep in their own thoughts.* **Szabo** *is practising with the puppet of* **Don Quixote**, *which waves a brave farewell to the audience.)*

(Curtain)

Idris Rowlands' Song

For - tune, my foe, Why dost thou frown on me?
And will thy fa - vours Ne - ver great - er be?

Frown though ye may, Yet shall you smile a - gain;

Nor shall my days Pass all in griev - ing pain.

Eros at Breakfast

Eros at Breakfast
A Psychosomatic Interlude

Characters:

Crito

Chremes

Aristophontes

Parmeno

Hepatica

(The setting suggests a superior departmental office; the stage is hung with curtains—a deep red for preference—and is carpeted with the same, or a complementary colour. The lighting is concentrated on the central acting area, so that the characters appear to enter from, and vanish into, shadow. At the back of the stage, and to the stage right, is a desk with a telephone on it, and the speaker of a communication system. There is a chair behind the desk and another, an armchair, in front and to the left of it; a sofa is to the left of this furniture. These furnishings should not suggest an ordinary office, nor yet the waiting room of an artistic dentist: something luxurious, and even plushy, but distinguished, is wanted.

Before the Curtain rises the audience hears part of the First Movement of the Classical Symphony by Prokoviev; after about forty bars there comes a climax which is the signal for the Curtain; the music then subsides, fading out altogether on cue.

When the Curtain rises, **Crito** *sits at the desk, examining some papers; he is a handsome young man, dressed in a uniform of subdued colour; it is an indoor, or palace uniform and no spurs, jackboots or other warlike appurtenances are needed; he has the air of a superior secretary; he hums softly with the music.*

Enter his superior, **Chremes**: *he is an older man, wearing the same uniform but with some differentiation—a star at the throat, or an order on the breast; his air is that of a diplomat and his bearing is distinguished.* **Crito** *rises courteously.)*

Chremes: Good morning, Crito. You seem to be in good spirits.

Crito: The best, sir; and you?

Chremes: Never better. How are the night reports?

Crito: Nothing uncommon, sir. A shade of excitement here and there, perhaps.

Chremes: You have reported from this department?

Crito: Everything in perfect order.

Chremes: Good. Routine—routine. Then we have nothing to do but wait for breakfast.

Crito: Excuse me, sir—did you mean to say anything?

Chremes: Eh?

Crito: A word to the observers, you recall, sir. *(He makes a gesture to indicate the audience.)*

Chremes: Oh, of course! How could I have forgotten? *(He steps forward and addresses the audience directly: his manner is that of a polished lecturer.)* Ladies and gentlemen: I am truly happy to appear before a group of such distinguished psychologists as yourselves; I see one or two of you shaking your heads deprecatingly at the word "psychologists"; shall we say, then, students of human nature? If you were not that, you would not be found in a theatre, where human nature is the principal stock-in-trade. Every playgoer is a psychologist. But however you may choose to describe yourselves, you are here to see something of the human soul at work. You smile: you think that I am pretentious—that I offer too much. How is it to be done? Well, for many years the workings of the bodily organs have had no secrets from medical observers, and the soul, at least in part, is the result of the working of the bodily organs. By observing the bodily organs may we not learn something of the soul, as well? Do I see a gentleman rising to leave? Perhaps he is a professional dealer in souls; pray be patient, reverend sir; remember that I promised only "something of the soul." The bodily organs and the soul are more closely linked than you may imagine, however; all life is miraculous. I think I see a sceptical smile on the face of that gentleman yonder who has the sleek look of a prosperous surgeon: he does not believe me because he has never cut the soul out of anybody— at least, that is what he thinks. I am prepared for scepticism, and indifferent to it. Frankly, I cannot take too much time to convince you that what I say about the soul is true, for I am not in a position to have any doubts about it. You see, I am part of a soul myself. . . . You are looking now into one of the departmental bureaux of the soul of a young fellow-townsman of your own. I won't tell you his name: that wouldn't be fair. We who work for and with him call him Mr. P. S. *(The music fades out completely about here.)* Those initials stand for Psyche and Soma—Soul and Body, or Spirit and Flesh—the two substances which make him what he is. The departmental bureau of Mr. P. S.'s soul into which you are now looking is called the Solar Plexus; his Oesophagus is just over there and his Stomach is just behind us. A great many of Mr. P. S.'s bodily and nervous processes are controlled from here. May I introduce myself? I am Chremes, the permanent head of this department. And this is Crito, my chief assistant. (**Crito** *bows from behind the desk.*) We are in constant touch with the other departments of Mr. P. S.'s system, of course. Will you tell the observers what is happening at present?

Crito: Certainly, sir. At this moment Mr. P. S., who has risen and dressed, is going downstairs to breakfast. In the Mechanical Department, which comes under the direction of this bureau, and which is situated just under where we are standing, everything is in readiness to receive and deal with a glass of orange juice, a bowl of a completely non-nutritious breakfast food which Mr. P. S. believes has exceptional energizing properties, two pieces of toast, one with marmalade and one without, and two cups of coffee.

Chremes: Thank you. Perhaps you wonder why Mr. P. S.'s descent of the stairs does not discommode us. Well, ladies and gentlemen, you live on a globe which is perpetually whirling at a speed of about sixteen miles a minute, and do you tumble down and roll about? What is going downstairs compared with that? Use is everything. Was that a report, Crito?

Crito *(who has been listening briefly to the telephone)*: A call from the Intelligence Department, sir. Mr. P. S.'s mother has run out of his favourite breakfast food and has told him that he must eat another—something which crackles and pops, the report says.

Chremes: Pay no attention; the Liver Department will complain if necessary. Mr. P. S. is twenty-one years old and it is Spring. What are explosive breakfast foods to us? *(He addresses himself to the audience again.)* Ladies and gentlemen, you realize, I hope, that you must not expect anything of a spectacular character: we work very quietly here, as a general thing. In ten or twenty years, perhaps, Crito and I may be confronted with some complicated and perhaps disagreeable problems, but at present all is routine—routine. The motto of Mr. P. S.'s school was *Mens sana in corpore sano*—a healthy mind dwells in a healthy body. I am not by any means sure that that is true: our Intelligence Department maintains that a healthy body is the product of a healthy mind, whereas we who belong to Mr. P.S.'s permanent Civil Service are convinced that without us neither mind nor body would fare very well. However, it is not my business to dispute about the matter at present. The important thing is that Mr. P. S. cherishes his school motto, and he still plays games now and then, and thinks himself athletic because he has not begun to grow fat. Though I must say that the way he eats—

Crito: Excuse me, sir: an official of the Metabolism Sub-Department assured me recently that Mr. P. S. will not put on weight for another ten years at least. Beyond that, he didn't like to say.

Chremes: Thank you. It isn't my job to speculate on such matters, of course, though I like to know about them. Well, ladies and gentlemen, I think that I have told you everything that you should know, and if you will excuse me, I shall go back to my work. *(He settles himself very comfortably in the armchair.)*

Crito: Are you expecting any calls this morning, sir?

Chremes: None in particular, but someone is sure to drop in. That is the beauty of a bureaucratic government such as this; constant visiting and conference between departments creates a pleasant air of bustle even when nothing out of the ordinary is being done. Bustle without fatigue: that is the essence of bureaucracy. Someone will drop in, mark my words. *(The telephone buzzes.)*

Crito *(speaking quietly into it)***:** The Solar Plexus: this is the Sub-Controller speaking. One moment, sir. *(Covers the mouthpiece and speaks to* **Chremes.**) The Intelligence Department: could you give Aristophontes a few minutes?

Chremes: Of course; with pleasure.

Crito: Happy to see you at any time, sir. *(Hangs up.)* There's your visitor, sir. Have you any idea what he may want?

Chremes: Nothing. Routine. Mr. P. S.'s Intelligence is not a demanding one. You recall how easily he got through his matriculation examinations?

Crito: Twelve subjects: three firsts, six seconds, two thirds, and a credit.

Chremes: And not a sleepless night or a bilious attack. There are people, you know, who have perpetual conflict and sometimes actual war between the Intelligence and the Solar Plexus. But not Mr. P. S. We may consider ourselves lucky.

(Music: the Second Movement of the Prokoviev. Enter **Aristophontes***: he wears a uniform like the others, but the throat of his coat is open, and under it he wears a dress collar and a white bow tie, as is the custom in the older universities: over his uniform he wears an academic gown, and he carries a square cap, vulgarly called a mortarboard, in one hand. He wears spectacles and has an academic manner, but not to any farcical degree.)*

Aristophontes: Good morning Chremes: good morning Crito.

Chremes: Good morning, Aristophontes. How is everything with you?

Aristophontes: Oh, routine—routine. We keep busy, of course, but really, so long as Mr. P. S. remains at the University there isn't too much for his Intelligence to handle. The professors are a very considerate lot, you know: they keep the actual thinking down to a minimum. If there were nothing before us except getting Mr. P. S. his Bachelor of Arts, I should be perfectly happy. You know him as well as I do: no doubts about religion; no doubts about politics—except for that week when he thought he was a socialist— no tiresome intellectual curiosity of any sort; a thoroughly solid young Canadian, in fact.

Chremes: Absolutely level-headed.

Aristophontes: Dead level. But there may be trouble ahead.

Chremes: Oh? Any signs?

Aristophontes: Poetry.

Chremes: I haven't heard anything about any poetry.

Aristophontes: The night before last Mr. P. S. was at a dance.

Chremes: I know.

Aristophontes: When he returned home he sat for thirty-five minutes on his bed, trying to compose some lines of poetry.

Chremes: We heard nothing of it, did we, Crito?

Crito: Not a word, sir.

Aristophontes: Well, you know it now.

Chremes: What are you concerned about, my dear fellow? It can't have meant anything if we had no part in it. The best poetry is written almost entirely under the guidance of the Solar Plexus.

Aristophontes: This was not the best poetry. And in Canada, my dear Chremes, damned little poetry is written from the Solar Plexus. It is squeezed out painfully by the Intelligence Department.

Chremes: Making bricks without straw; I know. You're fussing, Aristophontes.

Aristophontes: I am *not* fussing. When the implications of this business reach you, you'll change your tune.

Chremes: Go ahead, my dear fellow.

Aristophontes: At the dance, Mr. P. S. met a girl.

Chremes: He has met girls before.

Aristophontes: Not this girl. He was wearing his new evening dress suit, and you know what that means.

Chremes: It engenders a heightened sensibility in several respects, and sometimes produces delusions of grandeur. But the effects are seldom lasting.

Aristophontes: The wearing of dress clothes, among those who do so infrequently, refines and intensifies all the emotions. It arouses a crude ceremonial sense in those who ordinarily lack it; it makes the wearer of dress clothes more critical in his appraisal of others, but it also makes him more susceptible when his fancy is tickled. Mr. P. S. met a girl at the dance.

Chremes: Yes; go on.

Aristophontes: No. I merely thought I should let you know.

Chremes: Oh come: don't be so mysterious. What about this girl? Was he writing poetry about her?

Aristophontes: He *wanted* to write about her, but it didn't come out quite as he wished. Beginners at poetry, you know, must choose rhyme or reason: they can't have both. He plumped for rhyme, and every line pulled him farther away from the girl, whose name, by the way, is Thora. The poem ended up by being vaguely about Nature and the Universe, all because there is no really effective rhyme for Thora. Can you think of one?

Chremes: Hm. Thora? No. Can you, Crito?

Crito *(languidly)*: Bothersome Thora; how I deplore her.

(The actor must remember that although few Canadians would make this rhyme, **Crito** *is of the Soul.)*

Aristophontes: It's all very well for you to be facetious, but I see trouble ahead with this Thora.

Chremes: I tell you, Aristophontes, you're fussing. If Thora has created no impression in any of Mr. P. S.'s agencies but his Intelligence Department, it makes absolutely no difference if he has written an epic in nine cantos.

Aristophontes: You haven't heard everything, yet. He has sent the poem to her.

Chremes: But you said it was about Nature.

Aristophontes: You don't understand these matters, Chremes. Of course it is about Nature, if it's about anything at all—which is doubtful; but in such instances the poet simply calls it "To Thora," and puts the date on it, and the girl's Solar Plexus Department can usually be depended on to do the rest.

Chremes: Has Mr. P. S. done that?

Aristophontes: Yes, and he has sent it to Thora with a note saying that he hopes she won't mind, but he can't help it, and will she let him have a line to say she isn't angry!

Chremes: Angry? Why should she be angry? She isn't a critic, is she?

Aristophontes: No, no; and of course he knows she'll be pleased.

Crito: What hypocrisy!

Aristophontes: Not at all. If I may say so, you Solar Plexus officials are a little blunt in your approach to such matters.

Crito: If he likes the girl, why doesn't he say so? Why this shilly-shallying and verse-writing? Why not a direct declaration?

Aristophontes (*patiently, as one explaining to lesser intellects*): This year Mr. P. S. is taking an English course in the romantic poets: it has impressed him deeply: a fortnight ago he attended two performances by the Russian Ballet. He thinks flat-footed declarations of admiration unrefined, and so do the rest of us in the Intelligence Department.

Chremes: Oh, come off your high horse, Aristophontes. You're worried. You're afraid Mr. P. S. will fall in love with Thora.

Aristophontes: Yes, I am. And so would you be, if you knew everything about love that I do.

Chremes: Now don't pretend to be so knowing, Aristophontes. Mr. P. S. has never been in love and none of us can say what will happen when he is. It might be quite enjoyable. (*Phone buzzes.*) Was that a report, Crito?

Crito (*with phone to ear*): From below, sir. Breakfast not going too well.

Chremes: Humph! Ask for details.

Aristophontes: I hope this isn't going to mean trouble for you.

Chremes: Yes you do: you want to be justified in your gloomy forebodings. What's the report, Crito?

Crito *(still with phone, relaying the message)*: Mr. P. S. is listening for the postman: his mother has reproached him twice for not paying attention to what she is reading from the newspaper about world affairs: Mr. P. S. has a feeling that his mother lacks depth and understanding of life, and this has in turn created a sense of disloyalty and self-reproach which is inhibiting his digestion. *(He hangs up.)*

Aristophontes: Another of those rows with his mother!

Chremes: Unpleasant, of course, but not uncommon. I only hope it doesn't move him to self-pity; that raises utter hell in the intestines, and we don't settle down for days.

Aristophontes: I don't like it, Chremes. When a young man is about to fall in love, one of the earliest symptoms is a keen dissatisfaction with his mother.

Chremes: You've got Thora on the brain!

Aristophontes: Yes. That was very precisely stated.

Chremes: This is just Mr. P. S.'s usual wrangle with his mother. A boring woman.

Aristophontes: Oh, come. I can't admit that.

Chremes: Precisely. You fellows in the Intelligence Department can't, or won't, admit that Mr. P. S.'s mother is a bore. But we in the Department of Feeling and Intuition have known it for years. When Feeling is more accurate in summing up a situation than Intelligence, there is bound to be some uneasiness.

Aristophontes *(sententiously, as though repeating something he has said* *for years)*: Mr. P. S.'s mother is a Good, Kind Woman. She would do anything in the world for him. Remember how ill she was when she bore him. She is completely wrapped up in him—

Crito *(languidly)*: I wish she were dead.

Aristophontes: Crito! I won't hear such things! Do you hear! Chremes, discipline this Sub-Director of yours! If I am going to hear that sort of thing, I'll cut communication with this department!

Chremes: Oh stop fussing, Aristophontes! Your regard for Mr. P. S.'s mother is all rubbish.

Aristophontes: Rubbish!

Chremes: Crito spoke metaphorically. He simply means that he wishes that Mr. P. S.'s mother were safely and happily out of the way somewhere, and would leave the young man alone. *(Behind their backs* **Crito** *repeats quietly, "I wish she were dead.")* I'm sure we could all like her much better if she didn't insist that we love her.

Crito: I'll bet her Solar Plexus is a mess!

Aristophontes: I'm going! When you wish to apologize you can reach me in the usual way.

Chremes: Oh, sit down, Aristophontes! If we quarrel like this, Mr. P. S. will have trouble with his breakfast.

Crito *(listening to the phone)*: A report, sir: Mr. P. S. *is* having trouble with his breakfast. He is grumbling about the new breakfast food, as well. The fireman in the Epigastrium is hinting at heartburn.

Chremes: Really? It would be a shame if Mr. P. S. developed a dyspeptic tendency. Makes such a lot of extra work.

Aristophontes: Then be careful what you say. When the Intelligence and the Solar Plexus are at outs, anything can happen. And with this Thora business in the offing, we can't afford to have any gratuitous trouble.

(The **Intercommunication System** *speaks, suddenly and in a commanding voice.)*

Intercom: Attention, if you please! An envoy from the Heart!
(The music which follows this announcement is a Strauss waltz, preferably The Thousand and One Nights, *played softly and tenderly; it provides the background until cue to fade.)*

Chremes: Now, who can this be? And why doesn't he simply walk in like anyone else? Why this pompous announcement?

Aristophontes: And what music! The Intelligence Department decided several weeks ago that Prokoviev was Mr. P. S.'s favourite composer: what does this Heart fellow want with this vulgar, sugary Strauss?

Chremes: I still have a soft spot for Strauss. Who is it, Crito?

Crito: Probably Parmeno, sir. He hasn't been very important up to the present, but I hear that he is quite a power in the Heart now.

Chremes: Never heard of him. What the devil—

(From the dimness, Right, **Parmeno** *waltzes into the room. He is magnificently dressed in a hussar's uniform, with a pelisse, sabretache and every possible redundancy of military grandeur; his whole being speaks of romance; he wears no hat, and appears to be dressed for a ball. His hair and short side-whiskers are perfect; he might be Byron or Pushkin. As he dances,* **Crito** *hastens to move the chairs out of his way.* **Chremes** *and* **Aristophontes** *eye him without approval, the former cynical and the latter affronted.* **Parmeno** *comes to a stop at last, and when he speaks his manner and voice bear out his impression of romantic grandeur.)*

Parmeno: You expect me, I presume?

Chremes: There *was* a message that someone was coming from the Heart.

Aristophontes: A message and some deplorable music.

Parmeno: Exquisite music. The tender suspirations of romance. Which of you is in charge here?

Chremes: I am the Director of this bureau; my name is Chremes.

Parmeno: Indeed? *(Drawing himself up.)* I am Parmeno, the Envoy of the Heart. Who is this academic figure?

Chremes: A very important person from the Intelligence Department, Aristophontes.

Parmeno: So? You will both want to hear what I have to say.

Aristophontes: Frankly, I cannot imagine anything less likely.

Parmeno: It is useless to be hostile toward me. You will have to listen anyway. Now—I don't think you told me your name, Director?

Chremes: Is it possible? My name is Chremes; and my secretary is Crito.

Parmeno: So? Well, Chremes, we'll need your cooperation.

Chremes: In what?

Parmeno: In love, Chremes, in love! The divine, the adored one has come at last, Chremes, and the Heart of Mr. P. S. has capitulated and now lies in ruins—speaking figuratively, of course. At last we approach a Love Affair, a matter of the deepest significance, and every department of Mr. P. S.'s system must play its appropriate part. The Heart, naturally, will take the lead, and the direction of the Affair will come from that quarter. Other departments must be prepared to do whatever may be necessary at an instant's notice.

Aristophontes: One moment! Did I understand you to say that the Heart had taken upon itself to make this decision?

Parmeno: That is so.

Aristophontes: And what about the Intelligence, may I ask?

Parmeno: Love is not a matter of Intelligence, my good fellow.

Chremes: Love is a matter of Feeling. As Director of the Solar Plexus, I should like to know what you mean by making a decision of this sort without consulting me?

Aristophontes: Just a moment, Chremes. I haven't finished. Now, Parmeno, or whatever your name is, I won't be brushed aside. I'm accustomed to command in matters concerning Mr. P. S.'s general conduct—

Chremes: Don't exaggerate!

Aristophontes: Please! This talk of love is quite irregular. It hasn't gone through the appropriate channels of the Department of External Affairs.

Parmeno: Love, my good pedant, is not an external affair, but an internal affair.

Chremes: Quite. And why wasn't I asked about it?

Parmeno: Don't be hasty! You are being asked about it. That's what I'm here for.

Chremes: Do you call this asking? You came whirling into my bureau like a teetotum to announce an accomplished fact. You said that we all had to work with you—to take orders from the Heart.

Parmeno: And can you say no? Chremes, it is Spring, and two nights ago Mr. P. S. was at a ball—

Aristophontes: A dance—a stuffy little dance.

Parmeno: A ball!

Aristophontes: Mr. P. S. referred to it as "a hop."

Parmeno: Before he went; but now he thinks of it as "The Ball."

Aristophontes: Do you dare to tell me what he thinks? *(Seizes phone.)* Get me Intelligence—Files and Memorabilia: this is Aristophontes; read me the report on the *hop* two nights ago. *(To* **Parmeno.***)* You'll see! *(Again to the phone.)* What do you mean, *the ball*? Oh, the devil! *(Slams down the instrument.)*

Parmeno: You see? Now, as I said, Mr. P. S. went to the ball and after the seventh dance he saw her. She was dressed in white.

Aristophontes: Of the fifty girls at the hop thirty-six wore white frocks.

Parmeno: She wore a white gown. She had a gardenia in her hair.

Aristophontes: It was growing brown from the heat.

Parmeno: Do you wish to check that fact with your department?

Aristophontes: No.

Parmeno: That's as well. And now, will you permit me to continue without interruption? Thank you. He sought an introduction: he commented upon the fact that, while she had a gardenia in her hair, he wore one in his lapel, and she said, laughingly, "It looks like fate, doesn't it?" (**Aristophontes** *snorts.*) He asked for a dance: her program was filled. But ah! what sweetness! She crossed out a name and substituted his.

Aristophontes: It was her pimply cousin George's name.

Chremes: Be quiet, Aristophontes, I want to hear this.

Aristophontes: Chremes! Are you turning against me?

Chremes: Intelligence isn't the only way of finding things out, as every department knows but your own, Aristophontes. Go on.

Parmeno: They danced: they did not talk: it was a waltz.

*(He pauses for a moment, and the music of the waltz is heard, slightly louder than before. **Parmeno** closes his eyes in rapture. The waltz fades to nothing.)*

Crito: And was it then that he fell in love?

Aristophontes: That was when it first occurred to him that it would be fun to fall in love.

Chremes: Aha! Then you know more of this matter than you have admitted. Why wasn't I told? Crito, what was our report for the night of the ball?

Crito: One moment, sir. *(Reads from a day-book.)* General excitement and a rarefied emotion attributable to wearing evening dress. At 9:50 p.m. a sense of well-being caused by a drink of rye which a friend gave Mr. P. S. in the men's lavatory: this persisted until he lost his desire for food at supper-time: there is a note here that Mr. P. S. felt that eating was somehow unworthy of the situation in which he found himself.

Parmeno: You see? That was because he was having supper with Thora.

Aristophontes *(despondently)***:** Thora!

Parmeno: She yielded to his pressing insistence that she should have supper with him. He toyed with his food.

Aristophontes: Because he was talking and staring. Thora ate very efficiently, without seeming to do so.

Parmeno: He wanted to take her home, but she would not permit that: she had an escort. He walked home, breathing the scent of lilacs—

Aristophontes: And the exhaust of automobiles.

Parmeno: —And before he went to bed he poured out his heart in poetry.

Aristophontes: Oh, Parmeno, do have some respect for facts! He wrote sixteen very indifferent couplets.

Chremes: Not one of which caused the slightest tremor of the seismograph in this department. Mr. P. S. scribbled some doggerel: let us leave it at that.

Parmeno: How crass you are! Nevertheless, you will have to work with me from now on, and I hope that you will learn to look at this Affair in the only proper light.

Chremes: Very well. Let's see how we stand. Now, I am the head of a very practical department, as you know. Suppose this Love Affair goes forward:

what may we expect from it?

Aristophontes: Neglected studies, idling, daydreaming, and late nights.

Parmeno: The most exquisitely tender and innocent passages of first love.

Chremes: Innocent? How innocent? Mr. P. S. is twenty-one, and some people might think him a trifle slow for his age. I can't say that this department is concerned with preserving Mr. P. S.'s innocence, or Thora's either.

Aristophontes: My dear Chremes! Be prudent!

Chremes: You be prudent, Aristophontes; that is your job. Here in the Solar Plexus we have the continuation of the race to think about. You may depend upon it that if I commit myself to this Love Affair, I shall be just as imprudent as I can.

Crito: Oh, well said, sir! This begins to look like sport!

Chremes: It will play hob with our routine, Crito.

Crito: Who cares for routine! At last we're going to see some fun in this department! Hurrah!

(Music, loud enough to support the exhilaration of the moment: it is the Third Movement of the Prokoviev.)

Chremes: That's the spirit! Hurrah!

Aristophontes: Crito! Chremes! Recollect yourselves, for all our sakes!

*(Enter **Hepatica**, a beautiful young woman in a very becoming uniform; though lovely, she is extremely hard-headed.)*

Hepatica: Here! What's going on? *(The music fades quickly.)*

Crito *(catches her by the hands and waltzes her round the room)*: Oh Hepsie, my darling, we've caught a pretty little bread-and-butter Miss called Thora, and we're going to show her what she was made for! *(He sings.)*

What are little girls made for?
What are little girls made for?

Hepatica (*sings*):
Parties so gay, and rolls in the hay,
And that's what little girls are made for!

Aristophontes: Stop it! Stop it at once! It makes me shiver to hear you! Are you aware that Mr. P. S. is a member of a Continuing Presbyterian family?

Parmeno: Really, Crito, your attitude toward this matter is most unseemly. May I be presented?

Crito: Oh, of course. This is Parmeno, an envoy from the Heart. Hepatica, the Controller of Liver and Lights.

Parmeno: Gracious lady, permit me. (*He kisses her hand.*)

Hepatica: Hello, Parmeno; we haven't met before. You know the saying that there's a dash of woman in every proper man? I'm the dash in Mr. P. S.

Chremes: There should be a bit more dash in him from now on, Hepatica. Parmeno is here to tell us that we're beginning a Love Affair.

Hepatica: So that's it! I came up to ask a few questions. Down in my department they're secreting adrenalin at an astonishing rate, and as nobody ever tells me anything—

Crito: Hepsie, dear, I was going to call you the moment the conference was over.

Hepatica: This explains it, I suppose. The Liver is still the seat of the affections, you know.

Parmeno: Excuse me, the Heart—

Aristophontes: The Heart is the home of sentiment, you popinjay. There'll be no Love Affair without the Liver, and I think Hepatica will show more sense than you have, Chremes, with your base ambitions.

Chremes: Basic ambitions, old boy. *(In a voice of command.)* Crito, alert the lower centres!

Crito: At once, sir! With pleasure, sir!

Hepatica: A Love Affair! Oh good! Just what we want to liven things up!

Crito: I knew you'd see it that way. *(He gives an order by phone.)*

Hepatica: A Love Affair is worth a box of liver pills, to me. Do you know why so many athletes have liver trouble? It's because they misunderstand the nature of the Liver. All their thumping and banging and twisting and squirming is quite useless. Love may not make the world go round, but it's wonderful for the Liver. Thora will be just what my department wants; we'll make use of her in the Spring cleaning.

Crito: Good girl.

Hepatica: Oh, I know what *you* want.

Crito: And am I right?

Hepatica: Aristophontes will say no, but Aristophontes will have to listen to all the complaints and think up all the excuses if you get your way.

Aristophontes: Ladies and gentlemen, please: before this goes too far, let us listen to reason.

Chremes: That means listening to you, I suppose.

Parmeno: Surely everything is decided?

Aristophontes: No, no. Consider poor Mr. P. S. His year's examinations are drawing near. It is Spring.

Chremes and **Crito** *(with implications of conquest)*:	)
	)
Hepatica *(very businesslike)*:	) SPRING!
Parmeno *(ecstatically)*:	)

Aristophontes: Spring to you people means something entirely different. To me it means Mr. P. S.'s University career. Do none of you care whether he gets an education or not?

All: NO!

Aristophontes: Oh, how can you be so stupid!

Hepatica: You might as well understand, Aristophontes, that none of the other departments care a rap about education, in the sense in which you use the word.

Chremes: An extremely limited sense.

Aristophontes: That, if I may say so, is a deplorable attitude. With a good University degree, Mr. P. S. can be quite certain of a job in his uncle's stock and bond house. Oh, I'm not unreasonable! After eight or ten years of solid work and saving he can choose a wife—a girl of the highest type—and put her in a nice, cosy little home. They will love each other, and in time, if you people play your cards properly, there will be children—

Parmeno: Aristophontes, you disgust me! This young man has a Heart—

Hepatica: And a Liver—

Chremes: And a Solar Plexus—

Parmeno: All of which demand the sweets which youth can give. Your bond salesman in his sordid duplex with his sensible wife is an obscene blasphemy against the name of Passion—

Aristophontes: Oh, Passion, fiddlesticks! I know the world as you cannot. What I have described is what Mr. P. S. is headed for.

Hepatica: But is he to have nothing in the meantime? Must he wait for love until he can marry that nice, sensible girl who has had a job herself and knows that it takes a hundred cents to make a dollar, and a hundred dollars to have a baby?

Aristophontes: Why not?

Chremes: Aristophontes, I'll tell you why not. *(Breathing heavily and with meaning.)* Because you have disturbed my routine, that's why not!

Aristophontes: I? I did nothing.

Chremes: Well then, Parmeno or whoever it was.

Parmeno *(rapt)*: Oh Thora! Thora! I come to thee!

Hepatica *(matter-of-factly)*: Oh, Thora: by the way, haven't you forgotten something?

Crito: What?

Hepatica: Well, aren't you reckoning without Thora? Suppose she doesn't fancy our Mr. P. S.?

Chremes: Then he must make her fancy him! *(He unbuttons his tunic at the throat.)* He must seize her, dominate her, stifle her resistance with the heat of his passion!

Hepatica: I say, Cremes—steady! Your face is getting quite red.

Chremes: It was wrong to disturb my routine.

Aristophontes: Is it utterly useless to appeal to you?

Chremes: Utterly!

Parmeno: No use at all.

Aristophontes: Oh dear, oh dear! What a situation!

Crito: Oh come, sir. Why don't you come over to our side? Far more fun, you know.

Aristophontes: A Canadian's Intelligence is not an instrument of fun, Crito; it is a curb upon his baser instincts.

Parmeno: Baser? Baser, did you say?

Hepatica: You stinking snob, Aristophontes!

Chremes *(with menace)*: Do you want us to destroy you, Aristophontes? That often happens, you know, when the Intelligence becomes too overbearing toward the other departments. Sometimes it means disease, and sometimes madness, but it always means destruction.

Aristophontes: Oh dear! Forgive me. It's hopeless, I see. Do what you like. I give up.

Parmeno: Splendid!

Chremes: The best thing that you can possibly do.

Hepatica: Don't look so miserable. It'll be fun. You'll see.

Aristophontes: How shall I ever explain it?

Crito: I can help you out, sir. Don't explain it at all. Say it happened when you were drunk.

Aristophontes: Eh?

Crito: It's quite usual, I believe, to say that love is an intoxication of the senses; why shouldn't it intoxicate the intellect, as well?

Parmeno: Perfect!

Hepatica: You're a genius, Crito. Nobody blames a man for falling in love unless his reason seems to be in perfect working order.

Aristophontes: You mean—it will save my face?

Chremes: Come on! Let's have a party! Drinks for all, Crito!

(**Crito** *brings decanters and glasses from under the desk, and he and* **Chremes** *pour; the liquor might fittingly be of pretty and unusual colours.*)

Parmeno: A toast! To the divine, the adored Thora!

All: Thora! We adore her! *(They drink, with elaborate gusto.)*

Chremes *(solicitously)*: Do you feel anything, Aristophontes?

Aristophontes: Not much.

Chremes: Give him a bigger glass. (**Crito** *does so, and refills all the glasses.)* Now I'll give you one: to the Conquest!

All: Down with Thora! *(They drink again.)*

Aristophontes: Oh, deary me!

Crito: How is it now, sir?

Aristophontes: Hm! Nothing yet.

Chremes: Get him a really big glass. (**Crito** *does so.)*

Hepatica: Drink with me; to Love, which preserves the old and ripens the young!

(They drink, and **Aristophontes** *seems to swallow interminably as he drains a huge brandy glass.)*

Chremes: Crito, I believe there's someone on the line.

Crito *(at the phone)*: The Solar Plexus: this is the Sub-Controller speaking. Just a moment. *(To* **Aristophontes**) For you, sir.

Aristophontes: For me? 'Stror'nry. *(Strives to rise, and sinks again.)* Dear, dear; 'stror'nry deep sofa, this, Chremes. *(Tumbles back into it again, and giggles.)* Tell them go 'way.

Chremes: Aristophontes is engaged and cannot speak to you at present. What's that? Imperative? They say it's most urgent, sir.

Aristophontes: 'Sturgent? *(He sings: Tune "Reuben, Reuben")*
        Caviar comes from a virgin sturgeon,
        Virgin sturgeon's a very fine fish;

Virgin sturgeon needs no urgin',
That's why caviar's a very rare dish!
Whe-e-e-e-e!

Chremes: Tell them to put it on the speaker.

Crito: Will you put your message on the speaker, please. Yes, unavoidable, I'm afraid.

Intercom: Aristophontes: Sir: a most urgent message. The postman has brought Mr. P. S. a letter: he has it at the breakfast table now: the handwriting is feminine and runs downhill; the paper gives off a faint perfume. *(All inhale deeply.)* Mr. P. S. asks his mother for permission to read the letter: she assents, although her voice hints plainly that she is hurt because he has not said whom it is from; he cuts the envelope with a clean knife. I am going to cut you in on his heartbeat, sir. *(A rapid, throbbing drumbeat comes over the system.)* He reads, and what follows is a direct quotation, given in Thora's voice as he remembers it. *(Accompanied by the drumbeat, which grows slightly faster, a charming, sweet, unsophisticated girl's voice reads.)*

"Dear John: How sweet of you to send me that sweet poem. I read it twice and thought it was simply sweet. No one ever wrote a poem to me before and I don't know what to think. I certainly never thought I was the kind of girl to inspire a poem, but you never can tell, as they say. Of course you may see me again, you silly boy. Why not? After the ball and the poem, I mean.

(Strains of the waltz are heard, for a moment, and **Parmeno** *turns to* **Hepatica** *to dance, but she and* **Crito** *are clasped in a long kiss:* **Chremes** *broods triumphantly, and* **Aristophontes** *is listening in a melancholy stupor.)*

"Could you come around on Friday night, and we might go to the Dog Show. I love Airedales. Love, Thora."*(Male voice.)* That is all, sir.

Parmeno: Love! Love!

(Music: the Fourth Movement of the Prokoviev until Curtain.)

Parmeno *(declaiming)*:
>   What love is, if thou would'st be taught,
>   Thy heart must teach alone—
>   Two souls with but a single thought,
>   Two hearts that beat as one!

Hepatica: Nothing like love to whisk the Liver!

Aristophontes *(leaping to his feet)*:
>   Love is a nightmare with one foot,
>   Two children with one bun;
>   Two turnips with a single root,
>   Two cabbage-heads in one!

Chremes: Get him a larger glass!

Parmeno: She signs the letter, "Love—Thora." Oh, Thora, Thora!

Chremes *(rubbing his hands)*: Aha! Thora!

Hepatica *(indicating the audience)*: I say, what are all those? Don't you think they're learning a bit too much about Love?

Crito: Who can know too much?

(**Crito** *kisses* **Hepatica** *on the lips as* **Parmeno** *kneels to kiss her hand;* **Aristophontes**, *in despair, is drinking directly from the decanter;* **Chremes** *rushes forward to help close the curtains. The music is loud for a moment, and then fades to silence during, one hopes, the applause of the audience.)*

(Curtain)

Biography
Robertson Davies, Playwright

"Davies' dramatic strengths are witty dialogue, warm, humorous characterization, and thematic depth. . . [His] contribution to mid-century theatre surpassed that of any other playwright, and his dramatic quest for spiritual enrichment seems unlikely to go permanently out of date." (Susan Stone-Blackburn, in *The Oxford Companion to Canadian Theatre*)

One of Canada's most popular authors, Robertson Davies was born in Thamesville, Ontario, on August 28, 1913, and grew up there and in Renfrew and Kingston; he was educated at Upper Canada College, Queens' University, and Balliol College, Oxford.

Among his early books were two collections from his witty newspaper columns, "The Diary of Samuel Marchbanks," which gave him Canada-wide fame in the late forties. Davies first came to international attention with the Deptford Trilogy of novels—*Fifth Business*, *The Manticore* and *World of Wonders*.

But his first love was the theatre, starting with student productions at Upper Canada College and continuing through his university years. After graduate studies at Oxford, Davies joined London's Old Vic Company, where he acted, taught history of drama at the school, and did editorial work for the director, Tyrone Guthrie.

Soon after his marriage to Brenda Mathews in 1940, Robertson Davies returned to Canada as Literary Editor of *Saturday Night*. In 1942 he was appointed editor of the *Peterborough Examiner*.

Davies continued to be involved in theatre, mainly as playwright and director. He was awarded the Ottawa Drama League's playwriting prize for two consecutive years: in 1947 for *Overlaid*, and in 1948 for *Eros at Breakfast*. The latter also won the Dominion Drama Award for best production of a Canadian play, and the Gratien Gélinas Prize for best playwright. The Louis Jouvet Trophy was awarded to Robertson Davies in 1949 for his direction of *The Taming of the Shrew*, performed by the

Peterborough Little Theatre. *Fortune, My Foe* took the Gélinas prize that same year.

Over the next years several Canadian companies performed works by Robertson Davies. The Peterborough Little Theatre produced *The Voice of the People* in 1950, and *At My Heart's Core*, a three-act play, was commissioned for the Peterborough Centennial. The Crest Theatre in Toronto, which had been founded with a commitment to Canadian plays, premiered two of Davies' plays, *A Jig for the Gypsy* and *Hunting Stuart*.

Davies played a major role in establishing the Stratford Shakespearean Festival, arranging for his London friend Tyrone Guthrie to advise and direct the new Festival. Davies also worked to ensure the high standards for which the Festival is famous. Elected Governor of the Board of Directors in 1953, Davies served on the board from 1953 to 1971. He initiated and did most of the writing of the three books about the early days of the Stratford Festival, with the collaboration of Tyrone Guthrie and Grant Macdonald, Boyd Neel and Tanya Moiseiwitsch. More recently, his novel *World of Wonders* was adapted by Elliott Hayes for the Stratford stage in 1992.

In 1961 Davies was appointed the first Master of Massey College, a new graduate residential college of the University of Toronto. He taught in the English Department and the Drama Centre of the University and was visiting professor at Trinity College. On his retirement in 1981 he was named Founding Master of Massey College.

The top literary awards won by Robertson Davies include the Lorne Pierce Medal for literary achievement, the Stephen Leacock Medal for Humour, the Governor General's Award for fiction for *The Manticore*, the Toronto Arts Awards Lifetime Achievement Award, the Canadian Authors Association Literary Award for Fiction, and the Medal of Honor for Literature from the National Arts Club in New York. Davies' 1985 novel, *What's Bred in the Bone*, was short-listed for the Booker Prize, and his name was among the unofficial nominees for the 1992 Nobel Prize. His novels have been translated into seventeen languages.

Davies has received honorary degrees from twenty-one Canadian and American universities, Trinity College, Dublin and Oxford University, and was the first Canadian member of the American Academy and Institute of Arts and Letters. He is a Fellow of the Royal Society of Literature; Honorary Fellow, Balliol College; Member of the Order of Ontario; and a Companion of the Order of Canada.